PATRIOTS OFF THEIR PEDESTALS

PATRIOTS *off*
Their PEDESTALS

By

PAUL WILSTACH

Essay Index Reprint Series

BOOKS FOR LIBRARIES PRESS
FREEPORT, NEW YORK

STANDARD BOOK NUMBER:
8369-1738-3

LIBRARY OF CONGRESS CATALOG CARD NUMBER:
78-117862

PRINTED IN THE UNITED STATES OF AMERICA

To
STODDARD HANCOCK

It may be well to recall for such as would have their patriots prigs, that there was once a Spartan king who, while at play with some friends, remarked, on observing the approach of a coxcomb: "My friends, we must be grave, here comes a fool."—ANONYMOUS.

The cold marble influence of classicism appeared to have frozen the figures of the [Revolutionary and early Republican] period. They seemed in the grasp of a kind of historical self-consciousness. Public men disported themselves in movement and utterance as if they already felt under them the pedestal to which a grateful posterity would consign them. . . . The Revolutionary fathers left little undone to conceal the human glow underneath. They were, after all, in spite of their carefully concealed evidence to the contrary, flesh and blood, kind, gentle and generous, and must have been at heart fun-loving folk. They had eyes, hands, organs, dimensions, senses, affections and passions like their fellow-man; they were fed by the same food; hurt with the same weapons; warmed and cooled by the same summer and winter. If one pricked them, they bled; if one poisoned them, they died; but why in reason did they appear to wish it to be believed that if one tickled them they did not laugh?"—JEFFERSON AND MONTICELLO.

CONTENTS

PATRIOTS OFF THEIR PEDESTALS

PATRIOTS OFF THEIR PEDESTALS

THE IDEA

THE patriots on their pedestals are known, or should be known, or, at least, may be known to every one. That is why they are on their pedestals. The same patriots off their pedestals are quite another matter.

"Iconoclastic!" protests John Doe, ubiquitous critic, as well as sometime criminal; and Jane, his wife, echoes in a hopeful whisper.

On the contrary, an effort to know the fathers better, not to know them worse; an effort to know them off their pedestals, not to take them off; an effort to know them not in the austerity of bronze and marble, not merely aloft on granite bases, buttoned-up, head rigidly tilted as if in a photographer's clamp, hand in bosom or brandishing a sword, frozen in a pose, mute effigies without heart or blood; but as human beings in the actualities of life, unburdened by the problems of their public

13

careers, unrestrained by audience, relaxed and un-buttoned, in an occasional unguarded moment; an effort to listen and observe from a point a little nearer their elbow than their feet, certainly nearer than the foot of their pedestals.

In general, statuary and public monuments, as well as most methods of history, run rather too much to pedestal and too little to personality, and have thus made it somewhat difficult to get near our patriots of the ancient régime.

There are shaded paths in the Borghese Garden on the Pincian Hill of Rome that are lined with busts of the great Romans of antiquity and great Italians of a later period. About them there is no embarrassment of trappings. The heads and necks merge into merely a few inches of naked shoulder. The marble supports taper, and they do not raise the great men higher than eye to eye with the be-holder. In distinction to another type of monu-ment typified by the high and hideous pompacities of Victor Emmanuel which rear on lofty ornate pedestals in nearly every city in Italy, the Pincian busts bring their subjects very near. The whole presentment of character is simple and honest, con-centrated in the countenance. Wandering along those shaded paths one feels an awe tempered with ease, as if the marble eye would twinkle if it could, as if, if they could, the marble lips would speak and smile and leaven greatness with friendliness.

But even if one is imagined to stand at the foot of a pedestal and, looking up at the effigy of a patriot, say, as Jaurès said to Clemenceau, "You are not God," it need not mean, and it should not be implied, that one thinks so severely of him as Clemenceau conveyed in his reply to Jaurès: "You are not even the Devil."

To suggest an examination of heroic figures off their pedestals does not mean iconoclasm, derogation or an effort to pierce the armor of righteousness or to dim the halo of heroism. It is rather the friendly effort to come nearer. So far from indicating a disposition to serve as Devil's Advocate and find faults, the effort here is to balance the noble qualities of great characters with their amiabilities as fellow human beings.

It may be based a little on unbelief in the essential greatness of a pose; or, at least, a doubt of the complete convincingness of the reality of sculptors as translators of the whole character of a man in a single immutable attitude. It may in part be a little suspicion of the inadequacy, less of the sculptor than of his medium, doubt of the adequacy of stone and metal for expressing more than a phase of a character at most, and that in artificial terms.

Pedestals are apt to hold the subject up above an intimate gaze. They prevent a revealing acquaintance. They are important and expedient as symbols, as an aid to the unthinking, who are not readily capable of personal appraisal and receive definite impressions more easily from definite visualization. For this type of mind the bronze or marble effigy reveals a man as great in proportion to the height of his pedestal, to the superlativeness of its inscription, and even to the ornateness of the decoration. All these artificial aids to an unthinking man's impression are so many impediments to another kind of estimator.

The pedestals on which the great figures of other days are perpetuated for us are, however, not alone the architectural structures that support effigies in bronze and marble. It is because history has so often been written, however innocently, from the point of view of special pleader, and biography in an even greater average of cases has been written by enthusiasts who approached their subjects as preconceived heroes whose claim to greatness they feel it their duty to confirm in spite of anything and everything, that historians and biographers have been too generally pedestal-makers rather than sculptors of real figures.

Much history and much biography—there is a strong inclination to say most in both cases—is written with rather too much indifference to humor, which is at least as human as virtue, even if in impressiveness it ranks second to it. Some one has said that after the virtue in the world the fun in it is what we can least spare.

The fact that public figures have a personal character and a private life is what one misses in the bronze and marble effigies which have got themselves up on pedestals. There seems to be a popular attitude toward patriotic heroes which implies that the reputations of the revolutionary fathers might not survive a close-up; as if, with intimacy, their glory might fade and their grandeur might tarnish. In a word, it suggests that the less one knows of their private lives the more one will admire them. It would have the soldier forever in full dress on the back of a charger; a statesman in toga, arrested in the contemplation of scroll or tome, his brow wrinkled, but never his pants.

Revealing as is the public life of a great man as to his career, it is the peeps one has of his private

17

life that genuinely reveal and genuinely endear him. One of them is redeemed from being a lay figure by his passionate impetuosity, another by the infirmities of his temper, another by his domestic charm, another by his love of sports, another by his hobbies. It is a remote, unreal, great man who has no redeeming frailty.

The desire for intimacy is the flower of admiration. Does one admire Washington less because at times he stormed a little profanely, especially against ceremonials; or Jefferson less for the pitiful letters he wrote his negligent little daughter Polly begging her to write sometimes to her distant lonely father; or John Adams less for his hearty blustering indignation against humbuggery; or Chief Justice John Marshall less when in the dust measuring the distance of a quoit from a peg? Each one provides that touch of nature which gives kinship with the great.

One is more apt to find the real man when one finds him off his guard. If a gentleman is, as has been said, one who never unconsciously gives offense, it is equally true that the reality of any phase of character is revealed in unconscious moments.

He is a poor patriot and a frail hero who can

not be met face to face, in any of the actualities of his life. Contact should confirm perspective. It is difficult to hold the finer and deeper emotions for a theatrical figure, which is what so many hero-worshipers make of their subjects. One may admire the artist's technique; but what about his model, his subject, the figure behind the feat?

It may be remembered of the first biographies and histories written after the Revolution that theories of government and methods of administration were necessarily the engrossing interest of a young nation which had successfully emerged from one experiment and was just undertaking another. Measures were at the time more important than men, or at least men seemed important only as they stood related to the concept and administration of measures.

As that period retires into a more remote perspective its book of acts seems quite closed, but more and more curiosity grows as to the personalities behind the patriots. A little late it is found that there is no lack of military papers, nor public documents, nor of letters bearing on one or the other; but comparatively few sources of private intercourse with the fathers.

Fashions in literature were then almost as

austere as fashions in statuary and pedestals. Of
table-talk, private correspondence, the anecdotes
that they loved to tell or hear, or the anecdotes that
were told of them, there are comparatively few.
There was not a single Boswell to Washington,
Franklin, Henry, Hamilton, Adams, Jefferson,
Marshall or Madison. If much of their small talk
is so completely hidden as to have the reputation of
never having been, there is, nevertheless, a scrap
here and a scrap there, stray gossip, unconscious
self-revelation in occasional surviving letters, a few
diaries, side-lights giving insights, that seem well
worth skimming in an effort to find the humanities
of these apparently austere characters, and learn
if they may not really have been amiable as well as
admirable.

For all their detachment the public characters
themselves are curiously not less to blame than
their biographers. Victims themselves of the
marble and bronze ideal, they did what they could
to direct the chisel and the pen which were to define
them. Many of the early figures of our history
so completely edited the papers that they left behind as the witnesses of their character and acts,
that their earlier biographical portraits have since
been modified or even altered by the evidence which

that great detective, Time, has uncovered. They destroyed what evidence of their private lives they could. Comparatively few indeed are the surviving family letters of the public figures of the Revolution and the young Republic. They were especially careful to leave no possible correspondence between them and women, least of all with their wives.

If they tried to squeeze all the humanities out of their letters, their editors sometimes, if an Irish bull may be permitted, squeezed the rest. When Sparkes presented the first published collection of the writings of Washington, he corrected the General's spelling, his capitalization and his punctuation, and even touched up his choice of words and his habit of phraseology, so that the text emerged with a loss of much of the character and flavor of the natural original. This particular case of tampering was considered to have been so unfortunate that it was one of the justifications for the later edition of the writings of Washington edited by Worthington Chauncey Ford, who graciously allowed the General to be himself.

Gazing at these rigid features perpetuated for us in statuary, in engravings and in oil, it is legitimate to wonder did they never relax in smiles or break in laughter? Though they probably could not conceal it from their contemporaries, they seemed to be unwilling to admit to posterity that they had their gay and human moments, their sense of humor, and a willingness to play.

What did amuse them? When were they amusing? How did they divert themselves? What did they do when not acting on the public stage? What stories did they tell? What jokes did they laugh at? What diversions had they to relieve the serious business of booting kingship out of the country and of making a few million amateurs behave like a nation?

Herein are presented glimpses of eight of the most conspicuous of the fathers of the Republic. There is not one of them who is not safe on his pedestal from any consideration of his intimate life while off it. At this late date there is not a great deal that is new to be told of them. But much that is old and has long been submerged, is here rescued. Some, however, has not been even submerged, though believed to have hitherto been unused to point the personal and human traits of these several characters. Though much that is repeated here is known to delvers, and probably all might be, there are many general readers who may be sufficiently unfamiliar with what is here recalled, to make it an introduction to new as well as intimate and ingratiating phases of men who are to them more nearly heroic myths.

There actually was a lot of fun in the dear old boys in spite of their fear of its discovery and in spite of the dread of hero-worshipers that it would somehow reflect on their grandeur. To laugh with a man may exclude laughing at him. Has it not long been regarded as possible to love a man for his unconventionalities, that is to say his humanities? Is there not something honest and ingratiating in the invitation: "Draw near"?

I

GEORGE WASHINGTON

WASHINGTON was a good man and a great man, but he was not the prig that he has been made out to be. He was an aristocrat but not a snob. He had a sober sense of the block-and-ax business of leading a revolution against a king, but he had also a sense of humor. He had a sane appreciation of the dignity attaching to the formalities of the office of President, but he did not wholly like its social formula, against which he sometimes rebelled; and it did not prevent him from going to the theater, or from dancing as long as his legs supported him, or from drinking as became an old-fashioned American who still possessed and enjoyed the freedom he had fought for, or from pumping up a good sound temper on occasion and exploding it in terms of hearty indignation. He rode a horse well on a military march, in battle or on parade, but equally well over Virginia fields and fences when overseeing his own acres or when hunting the fox. His state and military papers are done in the starched and mannered English of his epoch, but there is evidence that at times he talked another kind of English, an English that sometimes dallied with anecdotes and at other times shot out like a fist.

One may not only "smile and smile," but, too, one may laugh and laugh and "be a villain still." No one of those near Washington, who handed his character down to us, seemed to think that the great man could even smile, much less laugh, and be a hero still. One of his biographers gravely stated that "during the entire seven years of the Revolution, Washington did not smile once." One would like to know how he knew, but he does not say. Irving, best of all Washington biographers, "detected a smile" at the battle of Trenton; a first crack in the falsely imposed veneer.

It was, I believe, in 1872, when the General had been dead three-quarters of a century, that an American historian devoted some considerable effort to proving that "Washington laughed." Up to that time such a belief, if it obtained at all, led a timid retired existence, lurking in the casual letters and anecdotes that rarely got themselves into the light, but belonged to the cave-dwelling clan of historical sources. They seem merely to have hibernated, however, for, when they were discovered, and dragged out, and the breath of life was blown into them, they, like certain hibernating animals, displayed a vitality which was quite vicious in its destruction of the cement in which some facts had hitherto been laid. The difference between history and historical sources is that the former contains just so much, or little, of the latter as the special pleader wants to use to prove his case. The case for Washington has been idealism pure and simple, in distinction to a sincere humanism.

Then so late as the date above, some one remembered that a Mrs. Allen had remembered this occurrence, without the now added italics:

"When Washington entered Boston, by what has been in consequence Washington Street ever since, he took up his quarters in what was then the Court boarding house, at the head of what we call State Street. It was kept by Mrs. Edwards. Mrs. Edwards' grand-daughter was a little girl, whom he would catch up, take on his knee and talk to. One day he asked her which soldiers she liked best, the red-coats or the blue-coats? The child was frank enough to say she liked the red-coats best. 'Ah, my dear,' said he, *laughing,* 'but they don't fight. The ragged boys are the boys for fighting.' Mrs. Allen had that story from her grand-mother. The *laughing* is essential to the anecdote."

The same narrator, remembering that Irving admitted a smile on the great man's lips on one occasion, believed *"he must have laughed"* at Princeton:

"When they saw some [enemy] cavalry broken and hurrying across country, Washington said to the gentlemen round him, 'A regular Virginia fox-hunt, gentlemen.' You don't suppose he said that as if he were at a funeral?"

Which drew from a candid commentator: "I confess that if he had refused to laugh at most of the jokes of those times, I should have said it was one indication more, that he was far in advance of his times." But jokes date. They rise and fall, and have their fashion and old-fashionedness, and, before lending a hand to the banner bearing the above legend, one might speculate on what our contemporary humor will be thought of one hundred years hence.

Surely there was sly waggishness, as well as edged tact, in the first President's greeting to his tardy guests on a certain occasion. He was a busy man and allowed it to be generally known that the hour named in an invitation to his table was the hour at which the company sat down. On one occasion a Congressman loitered in late, and found the party at table. Washington adroitly appeared to put the onus on his cook: "We are obliged to be punctual here. My cook never asks whether the company has arrived, but whether the hour has."

There was another kind of humor, a bit sardonic, disclosed by Patrick Henry, who saw Washington chosen by unanimous vote to be Commander-in-Chief of the Revolutionary Forces. Wise and human enough to anticipate eventualities, Washington, "with a tear glistening in his eye," said to Henry, "This will be the commencement of the decline of my reputation."

One lacking in a sense of humor would scarcely have handled another situation as Washington did, in the instance cited by General Mercer. It was during a sitting of the convention called to form a Constitution. The question up was the power to be given Congress in regard to a standing army. One of the members moved "that the standing army be restricted to five thousand men at any one time." Washington was chairman of the convention, and so could not offer a motion, but he whispered to another member at his elbow to amend the motion so as to provide that "no foreign enemy should invade the United States at any time with more than three thousand troops."

It is scarcely conceivable that there was not a good all around laugh at Mount Vernon, in which the General must have joined, when he drew up the one-year contract with Philip Bater, gardener, who, from the evidence in the document, was doubtless a good workman when sober, but was probably "half-seas over" most of the time. To correct this, Washington made an agreement whereby, in consideration of Bater doing his work well, and not suffering himself to be at any time "disguised with liquor," he would furnish to the dear drunk: "four Dollars at Christmas, with which he may be drunk 4 days & 4 nights;—a Dram in the Morning, & a drink of Grog at Dinner or at Noon."

An incident which, being wholly human, has been left in two varying versions, to cool its heels in the anti-chamber of history, gives, in the narrator's last line, an indication that it afforded Washington the heartiest laugh of which there is any record. Two youngish gentlemen had arrived on the General's estate to pay him a visit. They were his nephew, Bushrod Washington, later a Justice, and John Marshall, later a Chief Justice of the

Supreme Court. They had traveled on horseback, accompanied by a mounted black servant, who had the care of their luggage, a single large black portmanteau. The ride across the dry autumn roads had covered them with dust, so when they came to a creek, of which there were many on the many thousand acres of the Mount Vernon farms, and knowing there were no bathrooms in the big house, they stripped for a bath and a change into fresher clothes before presenting themselves at the mansion. When the black boy took down and opened the portmanteau, in the terms of one of the original chronicles:

"Out flew cakes of windsor soap and fancy articles of all kinds. The servant had by mistake changed their portmanteau at the last stopping place for one which resembled it, belonging to a Scotch peddler. The consternation of the negro, and their own dismantled state, struck them so ludicrously as to produce loud and repeated bursts of laughter. Washington, who happened to be out upon his grounds, was attracted by the noise, and was so overcome by the strange plight of his friends, and the whimsicality of the whole scene, that he is said to have actually rolled on the grass with laughter."

GEORGE WASHINGTON

One Archibald Robinson was in that procession of artists who came to "draw" the Washington portraits in such numbers that they wrung from the distinguished subject the plaintive admission:

"In for a penny, in for a pound, is an old adage. I am so hackneyed to the touches of the painters' pencils, that I am *now* altogether at their beck; and sit, 'like Patience on a monument,' while they are delineating the lines of my face. It is a proof, among others, of what habit and custom can accomplish. At first I was as impatient at the request, and as restive under the operation, as a colt is of the saddle. The next time I submitted very reluctantly, but with less flouncing. Now, no dray-horse moves more readily to his thill than I to the painter's chair."

By the time Robinson arrived Washington was broken to the chair, and in his case it was the artist who was "timid and worried." But to this situation we are indebted for the comfortable information that Washington eased the artist's embarrassment by inviting him to dinner at the family table, and "so delighted the company with humorous anecdotes that he completely set the table in a roar." There, truly, is at least one man's word for it that Washington indulged in anecdotes.

But where are the stories that he told? Gone, lurking in that limbo of the lost, but not damned. Not quite all, however,—with no thanks to Robinson, who gave no sample of the grave man's humor,—for one or two, from other sources, having served their sentence of solitary confinement, have come to light.

One of the rare survivors, which discloses the lowered reserve, without any of the gusto which sets a table in a roar, is told of a dare which Colonel Humphreys, secretary to Washington, and on a ride with his chief, gave him to jump a hedge. Washington accepted the challenge. The lively young officer was off first, cleared the hedge, but on the other side had the misfortune to find a muddy ditch which held his horse up to his girth. His challenged senior rode up to the hedge and discreetly looked over, and observed merely: "Colonel, you're too deep for me!"

Somewhat better, which it might perhaps be without effort, though it was told of the General and not by him, is a reply of his remembered by Doctor William Thornton: "As he sat at table after dinner, the fire behind him was too large and too hot; he complained and said he must remove; a gentleman observed that it behooved a general to stand fire; Washington said it did not look well for a general to receive it from behind."

His sense of humor cropped out in other ways. While in his twenties and off on the western frontier with Braddock, he wrote his "dear brother Jack": "As I have heard since my arrival in this place, a circumstantial account of my death and dying speech, I take this early opportunity of contradicting the first, and of assuring you that I have not composed the latter."

Though a young man when he wrote that, gaiety got into some of his letters, though a bit rhetorical, like the speech of his time, even to the end of his life. Within a year of his death he composed the following trifle for his wife to copy and add to a letter of her own to their friend, Mrs. Powell, of Philadelphia:

"I am now, by desire of the General, to add a few words on his behalf; which he desires may be expressed in the terms following, that is to say,—that despairing of hearing of what may be said of him, if he should go off in an apoplectic, or any other fit (for he thinks that all fits that issue in death are worse than a love fit, a fit of laughter, and many other kinds that he could name)—he is glad to hear *beforehand* what will be said of him on that occasion;—conceiving that nothing extra: will happen between *this* and *then* to make a change in his character for better, or for worse. —And besides, as he has entered into an engagement with M^r. Morris, and several other Gentlemen, not to quit the theatre of *this* world before the year 1800, it may be *relied upon* that no breach of contract shall be laid to him on that account, unless dire necessity should bring it about, maugre all his exertions to the contrary. —In that case, he shall hope they would do by him as he would do by them—excuse it. At present there seems no danger of his giving them the slip, as neither his health nor spirits, were ever in greater flow, notwithstanding, he adds, he is descending, and has almost reached, the bottom of the hill; —or in other words the shades below."

From the evidence of Washington's humor which survives there was about it little that was robustious. But, for that matter, that is not a quality usually associated with any great civil or military leader. Even Lincoln, who employed anecdote more than any other American leader, was as quiet as he was keen. Washington seems never to have lost the poise, which with him amounted to genius, except in indignation. He may indeed, as was once suggested, have well been "a man of violent passions held in magnificent control."

GEORGE WASHINGTON

Gilbert Stuart, who studied Washington's face at least as carefully and as expertly as any other man, said that he saw there the strongest passions possible to human nature. The actor, John Bernard, who should have been an accurate observer of such things, declared that his face disclosed signs of habitual conflict and mastery of passions. It was the "mastery" which fixed Washington's manner as well as his physiognomy, for no doubt the poise and coldness of his manner was the expression in part of this conflict and control. Certainly when he loosed his anger he was equal to fine fury and uncompromising oaths.

There is a story that when he met General Charles Lee at Monmouth, he asked him why his column was retiring. Lee said "the American troops would not stand the British bayonets." To which Washington whipped: "You damned poltroon, you have never tried them!"

One of Jefferson's favorite stories was of another such of Washington's outbursts, but that will appear later. It is not beyond belief that Washington used even stronger language than "Captain L——" reported in describing an instance of his making an aide "tremble like a leaf":

"It happened while he was President and travelling in his carriage, with a small retinue of outriders, from Mount Vernon to Philadelphia. It was during the first day of our journey, and we were passing through the barrens of Maryland, where, at intervals of a few miles, the solitude of the road was relieved at that time by a set of low taverns or groggeries, at which we did not think of stopping.

"But we had a thoughtless young man in our train, who by favour had been admitted into the family as a sort of gentlemen attendant, and who seemed much more inclined to patronize these places. The General, at his request, had permitted him to ride a favorite young mare which he had raised on his plantation, and of which he was exceedingly careful, the animal being almost as slight as a roebuck and very high spirited. But the young fellow, notwithstanding the intimations he had received at starting to deal gently with her, appeared bent on testing her speed and other qualities, and that too in a manner little likely to meet with favour in a man of Washington's high sense of propriety.

"He would leave the train, and riding up to one of the liquoring establishments, there remain until we were out of sight; when he would come up upon the run, ride with us a while, and gallop on forward to the next. This he repeated three times, the last of which brought the mettlesome creature to a foam and evidently much fretted her.

"At the first transgression thus committed against the General's orders respecting the mare, as well as against his known sense of propriety, he seemed surprised, looking as if he wondered at the young man's temerity, and contented himself with throwing after the young man a glance of displeasure.

"At the second he appeared highly incensed although he said nothing, and repressed his indignation, acting as if he thought this must be the last offense, for the punishment of which he chose a private occasion.

"But as the offender rode up the third time, Washington hastily threw open the carriage window, and asking the driver to halt, sharply ordered the former alongside; when with uplifted cane, and a tone and emphasis which startled us all, and made the culprit shake and tremble like a leaf, he exclaimed, 'Look you, sir; Your conduct is insufferable! Fall in behind there, sir; and as sure as you leave us again, I will break every bone in your skin!' "

Indeed we have Washington's own words for

the matter of his temper. At his table one day
General "Lighthorse Harry" Lee, who seems to
have been equal to any degree of candor with the
old sweetheart of his mother, quoted Gilbert Stuart
as having said that the General had a tremendous
temper. The General was silent, but Mrs. Washington came to the breach with: "Mr. Stuart took
a great deal on himself." Lee, to ease the situation, then amended that Stuart had added that the
General had his temper under wonderful control.
Whereupon Washington smiled, and remarked:
"Mr. Stuart is right."

Although his political enemies wrote of his coldness, his aloofness, his aristocratic manner and
bearing, he seems to have been a gentleman who
simply wanted "no nonsense," in the futile meaning of the word. His account books and letters
show that he had a sound notion that there was a
false economy in cheapness, but that, though he
generally asked his English agents to send him
what was fashionable, he was no dabster for
fashion, as, for an example among many, this order
on London for a French felt hat attests: "I do not
wish by any means to be in the extreme of the
fashion, either in the size, or in the manner of cock-
ing it."

He knew how to be simple, but he made no pose of simplicity, nor would he use it to offend another. There were twelve horses in the President's Philadelphia stables, for travel, ceremony and exercise; but, for all of them, and his fondness for them, and the aristocratic background they provided, he did not scorn to walk, to market for his own table, or, at times at least, to carry home his own purchases.

"Once," a Philadelphian remembered, as he had seen the occurrence, "Washington walked among the fishstands at the foot of Market Street.

" 'Auntie, that is a fine shad you have there,' pointing to a fine one in the fisherwoman's basket.

" 'Yes, General, let me send it home for you.'

" 'No,' said he, 'put a string through its gill. I reckon a man can carry home his own grub.'

"The good woman, therefore, tied a string through the gills, and off the General started with his fish in one hand and his cane in the other. As he passed along towards his home at Sixth and Market Streets, he found for once that he had undertaken more than he could accomplish; for at every step a hat would be raised in his honor, and of course the General's was to be removed in response. This he found was no easy task, but he soon solved the difficulty by putting his hat under his arm, and was thus able to bow bareheaded to those who saluted him."

The difference between his pedestal and his privacy finds its illustrations in several other instances. Nowhere, possibly, more definitely than on his trip home from Philadelphia when he had finished his second term in the Presidency. The way was made gala with banners and buntings, crowds and bands of music and addresses, at every city and at every settlement on the way. No doubt the President looked very dignified and responded with becoming seriousness; as properly he might. But while the populace thought only of the demi-god who had passed their way, he thought only of the furniture and furnishings left behind in Philadelphia, the condition of his house ahead of him at Mount Vernon as he would find it, and meanwhile he was pretty uncomfortably crowded in his coach.

Between oratory and fanfares and flag-waving, along the way from the Schuylkill to the Potomac, he wrote letters to his Secretary, Tobias Lear, left behind in the then capital, only of what seems to have been uppermost in his mind.

From Chester: "To give the greater surety to the large looking Glasses, and such other articles as are liable to be injured by the jolting of a dray;

be so good as to have them taken down by hand, and stowed where they will not be trod on; or tossed about in the Vessel's hold.

"The grate (from M^r. Morris's) pray have packed first in some old Carpeting to keep it from scratching. . . .

"I question whether enough of the small hooks were got; —desire M^r. Dandridge to get a couple of dozen more, like the two he took out of my Room yesterday."

More parades and speeches at other towns below, and then another letter, from the Head of Elk:

"Let me request you to provide for me as usual *new* Carpeting as will cover the floor of my blue Parlour. That it may accord with the furniture it ought to have a good deal of blue in it; —and if Wilton is not much dearer than Scotch Carpeting—I would prefer the former. All the old Carpeting (belonging to me) I would have sent; —and Mrs. Washington requests that you would add the Bellows and the Vessels (Iron & Tin) in which the ashes are carried out. . . .

"Pray get me of those Thermometers that tell the state of the Mercury within the 24 hours. Doctor Priestly or M^r. Madison can tell where it is to be had. Perhaps the old one if no thing better, may do to present to M^r. Snowden. . . . '

More public adulations to the hero at Baltimore, whence he despatched another of the sequence of errands for Lear:

"The furniture belonging to the public ought to have been well cleaned, as well as the Rooms before they were turned over to the President's order, with the Papers.

"Let me request the favour of you to purchase for me half a dozen pair of the best kind of White Silk stockings (not those with gores but) to be large, and with small clocks (I think they are called) I want the same number of raw silk, for boot stockings; large and strong."

But it seems other demands are made of a great man than to be serenaded and addressed and cheered, for in a postscript to Lear is a thumbnail sketch of conditions inside the coach in which the great man traveled:

"On one side I am called upon to remember the Parrot, and on the other to remember the dog. For my own part I should not pine much if both were forgot."

Washington's entire life at Mount Vernon points his love of the out-of-doors, of riding, hunting and fishing, as well as of music and of dancing within. His record for dancing endurance, in spite of what is probably a pardonable exaggeration, seems to have been made on the occasion noted by General Greene in a letter, from camp in New Jersey, to Colonel Wadsworth:

"We had a little dance at my quarters a few evenings past. His excellency and Mrs. Greene danced upwards of three hours without sitting down. Upon the whole we had a pretty little frisk."

No great stress has been laid on the curtain lectures Washington is believed to have endured from Martha, his wife. One of these has been reported by a guest at his house, however, with some particularity, which not only clinches the fact of the curtain lectures but proves as well as anything else that is told of him how well Washington could, if he had to, keep his temper. On that occasion the General and Mrs. Washington were in a room separated from the visitors by a somewhat thin partition, and Martha's voice penetrated to the listeners. The eavesdroppers did not disclose the details of her discourse. They allowed it to be known, however, that she was not interrupted by her husband until she had finished, when he was heard to say merely: "Now, good sleep to you, my dear."

Martha and her granddaughter, Nellie Custis, seem to have kept Washington's life rather well filled with one thing and another, as seen from his hint of the dog and the parrot and himself in the coach; and the man who could manage armies at least once confessed his weakness in managing women. When one of his nephews was proposed as superintendent of Mount Vernon estate, Washington was cool to the suggestion, replying incidentally:

"But after all is not Lawrence Lewis on the point of matrimony? Report says so, and if truly, it would be an effectual bar to a permanent establishment in my business, as I never again will have two women in my house when I am there Myself."

But, in this connection, the joke was on the General after all. Lawrence Lewis did not come to Mount Vernon as superintendent, but Martha married Nellie Custis to him, (the young man "relinquished the lapp of Mars for the sports of Venus," were Washington's words in writing of it to Pinckney) and during the General's and Mrs. Washington's lifetimes the young couple never lived permanently anywhere else than under that roof. Once when Lewis was temporarily absent, Washington, in writing him, hinted to him in delicately veiled terms that it was time for him to establish himself and his wife elsewhere. He named generous terms by which a great tract on the west side of his own estate should be at the disposition of his nephew until his own death made it over by his will. Lawrence seems to have taken the land, but not the hint. Washington, in spite of himself, had "two women in his house" till he died.

Washington was farthest from his pedestal and nearest our hearts on his last day out-of-doors. It was a gray December day. As usual he spent the hours, between breakfast and the old-fashioned mid-afternoon Virginia dinner hour, on horseback riding over his farms. On such rides he wore a suit of gray homespun, a greatcoat with high turned collar, a broad brimmed hat, and carried an old umbrella lashed to his saddle.

He left the mansion, on such inspections, about ten and returned about three. While he was out, on this occasion, the weather changed, and rain and snow and sleet drove down on him alternately, before a raw cold wind. But the old spartan spirit was still strong. He neither abridged his ride in the face of the storm, nor did he even raise his umbrella.

He plodded on, regardless of snow and wind, himself and his horse a white apparition. He reached the mansion coated with sleet. He laid off his greatcoat but could not be persuaded to make any further change of clothing.

Four days later, however, the last Collector took his toll of such custom and such courage. Earlier in that autumn Washington was left the sole survivor of all his father's children, and, remarking it and sensing the approach of the inevitable, he had said:

"When I shall be called upon to follow them is known only to the Giver of Life. When the summons comes I shall endeavor to obey it with good grace."

He did.

II

BENJAMIN FRANKLIN

BENJAMIN FRANKLIN and George Washington, generally accredited the two foremost characters of eighteenth-century America, although twins in their love of liberty, in their devotion to the liberation of the colonies and to the establishment of the new nation, as well as in their appreciation of each other, were as dissimilar in personality, in character and habits, as it were well possible for two equally eminent figures to have been.

Even though Washington was by no means the "grand, gloomy and peculiar" demigod that was cemented in the foundations of the national consciousness of him, he was a figure of reticence and distinction. Franklin, though a philosopher and statesman of the first order, was approachable, affable, companionable and a sage wag.

Washington was a country boy; Franklin a town boy. Washington was particular and elegant in his dress, equipments and environment; in such matters Franklin was careless and indifferent. Washington was conventional and a conformist; Franklin was unconventional and a non-conformist. Washington has been accused of having had a slow, plodding, one-track mind; no one ever denied that Franklin had a mentality like a scintillating comet throwing off sparks as fast as it traveled.

Washington was habitually grave, but knew how to be gay; Franklin was habitually good-humored and sprightly tempered, but none knew better than he how to be as serious as he was profound. Washington was domestic, Franklin was cosmopolitan. Both men were devoted to women; but Washington sought a wife, and Franklin, though he did marry, and became a family man, seemed well enough satisfied with mistresses. Both wrote maxims. Washington's were called Rules of Civility; Franklin's were embodied in the Sayings of Poor Richard. The General honored his in the observance; the Doctor honored his in the exception.

Yet such was the catholic nature of each that he appreciated the other without reservation, and so proclaimed unfailingly and unflinchingly. Toward the end of both their lives they reflected the "mettle of their pasture" in two letters which

passed between them. Franklin, in the year 1789
and the next to his last year, wrote Washington:

"My malady renders my sitting up to write
rather painful to me; but I cannot let my son-in-
law, Mr. Bache, part for New York without con-
gratulating you by him on the recovery of your
health, so precious to us all, and on the growing
strength of our new government under your administration. For my own personal ease I should
have died two years ago; but though these years
have been spent in excruciating pain, I am pleased
that I have lived them, since they have brought me
to see our present situation. I am now finishing my
eighty fourth year, and probably with it my career
in this life; but, in whatever state of existence I
am placed hereafter, if I retain any memory of
what has passed here, I shall with it retain the
esteem, respect and affection with which I have
been, my dear friend, yours most sincerely."

Washington replied immediately and at greater
length, and, after acknowledging Franklin's con-
gratulations and expressing a tender sympathy
with his feeble condition, concluded:

"If to be venerated for benevolence, if to be admired for talents, if to be esteemed for patriotism,
if to be beloved for philanthropy, can gratify the

human mind, you must have the pleasing consolation to know, that you have not lived in vain. And I flatter myself that it will not be ranked among the least grateful occurrences of your life to be assured that, so long as I retain my memory, you will be thought of with respect, veneration and affection by your sincere friend."

There is another, and perhaps the most significant, distinction between these two patriots. Though the last few decades have seen some efforts, not wholly unsuccessful, to unstarch the traditional Washington, to rehumanize and reclaim a quite human being, Franklin's reputation has crystallized entirely in quite the opposite way. It is precisely for Franklin's humanities that nearly every one knows him: for his universal curiosity, his homely scientific experiments and deductions and inventions; as a printer, an almanac-maker, as a friend of women and as the discoverer of the lightning-rod. He is, indeed, in most minds more nearly identified with Poor Richard than with his greater sterner self.

Where, then, in the stodgy little frame in its simple cloth suit, where, behind the round jovial face of the joke-smith and the jack-of-all-trades, — of whom it is reported that his confrères did not ask him to write the Declaration of Independence because they were afraid he might put a joke in it,—is the starch and spine of the patriot, the diplomat, the nation-builder, who in popular consciousness never quite elbowed Poor Richard off the pedestal?

Franklin lived eighty-four full years, from 1706 to 1790. Of these years he served his fellow citizens forty-nine years in public office, and his public services are estimated, among all the eighteenth-century patriots, as second to those of Washington only. Of these forty-nine years in public office twenty-five, incidentally during the last thirty-three of his life, were spent out of his own country, then little settled and civilized, in France and in England, at the time the two most urbane and cosmopolitan countries in the world. Yet he did not lose sight of his fellow colonists' point of view. Even when most fêted and acclaimed abroad, he was not less an American, or less zealous or less successful in advancing the colonial interests in diplomatic and economical negotiations with the first minds of the kingdoms of England and France.

Franklin the politician was born when, in his early teens, he formed, in Philadelphia, a secret club called the Junto, a close corporation of only twelve members. It was something between a Rotary Club and Tammany Hall, mantled over with the practical cast of both of them. His own most significant statement of the workings of the Junto appears in his *Autobiography:*

"We had from the beginning made it a rule to keep our institution a secret, which was pretty well observ'd; the intention was to avoid applications of improper persons for admittance, some of whom, perhaps, we might find it difficult to refuse. I was one of those who were against any addition to our number, but, instead of it, made in writing a proposal, that every member separately should endeavor to form a subordinate club, with the same rules respecting the queries, etc., and without informing them of the connection with the Junto. The advantages proposed were, the improvement of so many more young citizens by the use of our institutions; our better acquaintance with the general sentiments of the inhabitants on any occasion, as the Junto member might propose what queries we should desire, and was to report to the Junto what passed in his separate club; the promotion of our particular interests in business by more extensive recommendation, and the increase of our influence in public affairs, and our power of doing good by spreading thro' the several clubs the sentiments of the Junto."

It is not surprising that this simple and adroit means of feeling the public pulse, as well as for regulating its beat, had not been long established before its author and chief was drawn into public life; that, in 1736, he was made Clerk of the Assembly of the Pennsylvania Colony, and Postmaster of Philadelphia in the year following; that he was returned to the Assembly year after year; or that, once he got into politics, he never got out of it. He had not meanwhile neglected that other most efficient wheel-horse of a political career, a newspaper, but had fortified himself with the ownership and editorship of the *Pennsylvania Gazette*.

But the point about this remarkable man is that, though one of the shrewdest and most adroit men of his century, he also commanded within himself extraordinary resources of philosophy, humor, tact and vision, as well as bravery and persistence, and so leavened them with pure patriotism for the cause of liberty, that he rose inevitably from the plane of politics to that of statesmanship, and he readily drew the acclaim of two continents and all his contemporaries.

PATRIOTS OFF THEIR PEDESTALS

Apprehending a war with France for the territory behind the Atlantic littoral, "The Lords of Trade," in 1754, assembled a congress at Albany representing the different colonies. As a member for Pennsylvania, Franklin there raised himself to a "national" position by securing the adoption of his plan, which was nothing less than the first suggestion of that policy of union which has ever since been our national bulwark. He even appeared with a slogan which gave a digest of his plan, and the consequences of its rejection, in three words: "Unite or Die!"

If anything else had at the time been needed to further that expanding reputation, it might have been found in a letter which he despatched privately to an acquaintance in England. Intended to dishearten the British, it might well have been broadcasted to hearten the Americans. "The English have made a campaign here," he wrote, "which cost two million; they have gained a mile of ground, and lost half of it back again. They have lost 1,500 men and killed 150 Yankees. Meantime we have had between 50,000 and 70,000 children born. How long will it take to conquer America?"

Curiously, his political career so far seems a mere by-product of his thought and action. He uses it sometimes to promote his unselfish civic plans, but for the most part his activities are his business of printer and publisher and the schemes of his restless, inquiring, acquisitive, universal mind. From the time he entered public life in 1736, until he left America on his first foreign mission, he created a fire-department for hitherto unprotected Philadelphia; he founded the American Philosophical Society which survives to-day; he invented the open-face or Franklin stove, known and used even in this generation; he helped to found the University of Pennsylvania; he promoted a City Hospital; he introduced street paving and street cleaning in Philadelphia; he started a magazine for all the colonies, for which, however, they were not yet ready; he conducted electrical experiments with "kite and key," and otherwise, which made him the scientific marvel of the public and of the scientists of France before he even went there; he invented, and caused to be installed, the four-pane street-lamp with air vents above and below; he discovered the method of improving the soil with lime; he created the first penny-post in the colonies, at the same time extending routes and services and opening the mails to all newspapers; and he proposed a voluntary militia, which he organized, of which he was offered and declined the colonelcy, which he financed with a lottery, for which he designed insignia and mottoes and built a battery, and which he supplied with cannon for the defense of Philadelphia. One can almost hear him chuckle as he wrote of how he and others came to get the chief quota of cannon which were lent by Governor Clinton of New York:

"He at first refus'd us peremptorily; but at dinner with his council, where there was great drinking of Madeira wine, as the custom of that place then was, he softened by degrees, and said he would lend us six. After a few more bumpers he advanc'd to ten; and at length he very good naturedly conceded eighteen."

Franklin's diplomatic career began in 1757 when the Pennsylvania colony sent him to England as its agent to require the Proprietary, residing in England, to pay taxes on the annuity they drew from the colony. He remained five years, and was again returned by Pennsylvania in 1764 to prevent the operation of the Stamp Act. At the same time other colonies made him their London agent, and, before he returned home in 1775, he was generally regarded as the agent abroad of all the American colonies. For fifteen out of seventeen years he was virtually the ambassador of the fretting, then seething, and finally rebellious colonies; yet an ambassador without the prestige and backing of a country; for he stood "for a nation uncreated, for a congress without power"; alone, separated from his base by the most primitive communications at a time when it required six months to send a letter across the Atlantic and receive an answer to it; arguing causes where they were most unpopular, single-handed before the King, the Privy Council, the Cabinet and the Parliament of the most powerful nation on earth. In 1776, when the American colonies declared themselves independent of Great Britain, Franklin was put on a ship and sent across the ocean for another nine years, this time to France, as Commissioner to secure national recognition and other things, and later as first Minister after having secured recognition of the American states as an independent nation.

These twenty-five years of foreign service boiled down disclose an astonishing result. With reservation only of extent, the parings in some cases of the shrewd bargainer who overcharges and yields grudgingly as far as the price he secretly determined on; surmounting snubs, breaking down precedent, overcoming difficulties at every step;

the joker, the almanac-maker, the scientific experimenter, the obvious yet to so many the inscrutable little round man with the placid round face, achieved every single errand on which he set out.

The English proprietors of Pennsylvania were made to pay taxes; the Stamp Act was abolished; he made a treaty with France recognizing our national entity, secured French loans, obtained the privilege of fitting out privateers in French ports, and finally drew France into the War for Independence as our ally. Starch and spine enough here.

The requisites of a diplomat have been enumerated by one John W. Foster, Secretary of State under Benjamin Harrison, as "a conciliatory temperament, a spirit of expediency, business capacity, ability to gain the friendship and confidence of men of influence and standing, great popularity in social circles, a favorite diner-out." Franklin possessed them all.

Shelbourne, British Prime Minister, said: "Doctor Franklin knows very well how to manage a cunning man, but when the Doctor converses or treats with a man of candor there is no man more candid than himself."

And he had other requisites. A Secretary of

State is credited with having said: "We can send an Ambassador to Spain who does not speak Spanish; we can send an Ambassador to Italy who does not speak Italian; we can send an Ambassador to France who does not speak French; but we cannot send an Ambassador to England who does not speak English." Franklin was one of the most accomplished English scholars of his time.

Haled before the Privy Council on one occasion, he stood on his feet for an hour to receive the abuse of the Attorney General of England. His silence was heroic. Walpole made it the occasion for an epigram:

"The calm philosopher without reply,
Withdrew, and gave his country liberty."

Franklin knew, for he said, that "he who spits against the wind, spits in his own face." Of that rating before the Privy Council he later wrote: "I made no return of the injury by abusing my adversaries, but held a cool and sullen silence, reserving myself to some future opportunity." It is pertinent to remember that on this occasion the Doctor wore a new suit of spotted Manchester velvet, which was to be worn again, when his "future opportunity" finally did arrive.

When he was examined before the British

parliament in connection with the consideration of
the Stamp Act, his conduct of his case raised to its
highest point his political reputation in Europe,
and caused Burke to say that it reminded him of
"a Master examined by a parcel of school-boys."

It takes nothing from his resourcefulness that
he was acute enough to make friends among the
Members and by prearrangement slyly induced
some of them to ask certain questions for which he
had pat replies containing precisely the information
and arguments that he wished to have spread before the Crown and Court and Commons.

His genius for crystallizing a cause in an
epigram had been more than hinted in his long list
of *Poor Richard's Sayings,* as well as when, at the
Albany Convention, he introduced the pithy and
prophetic motto "Unite or Die!" On his first
mission to England he put the whole case of the
American colonies in four lines: "The sovereignty
of the Crown I understand. The sovereignty of
the British legislature out of Britain I do not
understand. We are free subjects of the King;
and fellow subjects of his dominions are not
sovereigns over fellow subjects in any other part."

When he was called before the British Parliament on the question of the temper and the

possible pacification of the colonies, it required spinal as well as cerebral strength to stand alone and declare: "The Parliament has not, never had, and of right never can have, without consent given, either before or after, power to make laws of sufficient force to bind the subjects of America in any case wherever, and particularly in taxation. We are free subjects of the King, and fellow subjects of his dominions are not sovereigns over fellow subjects in any other part."

There was candor, and it was backed by the resolution expressed by him openly at the same time: "I have some little property in America. I will freely spend nineteen shillings in the pound to defend my right of giving or refusing the other shilling. And after all, if I cannot defend that right, I can retire cheerfully with my family into the boundless woods of America, which are sure to afford freedom and subsistence to any man who can bait a hook or pull a trigger."

In spite of such utterances it is amusing to find him writing home: "I find myself suspected of my impartiality, in England of being too much an American, and in America of being too much an Englishman."

In the midst of Parliamentary hazing and

Privy Council attacks in England, and attacks on his income and abuse from rival patriots as well as rival editors at home, Franklin did not lose his good humor, his good sense or his love of living. During these English years he had a hundred other interests besides his diplomatic errand, though many of these very interests contributed to his efficiency in doing it. He experimented in electricity and musical glasses. His inventions included a stove that would consume its own smoke and a reformed alphabet and phonetic spelling. He not only changed the mind of Parliament but actually recommended a scheme for changing its air. He advanced the notion of daylight saving, though the phrase and the fact came more than a century later. He advised the English to put lightning-rods on Buckingham Palace, St. Paul's Cathedral and the government powder magazines.

Everything interested him and his pen from drowned flies, the effect of deep and shallow water on the speed of a boat, and seeds and animals for the Pacific islands, to the Gulf Stream, the Northwest Passage, the aurora borealis, rainfalls and swimming, and even the practical application of "oil on troubl'd waters." He traveled all over England and Scotland, France, Holland and Ger-

many. Oxford and St. Andrew's between them
made him twice a doctor. He enjoyed the devil-
tries of the Hell Fire Club in addition to the good-
fellowship of other clubs. He advanced his
mission by incessant letters to the newspapers, even
hoaxing the nation with the preparation and publication of an edict reputed to have been issued by the
King of Prussia.

Franklin returned to Philadelphia in the spring
of 1775. He was at once made a delegate to the
Second Continental Congress. He was not
eloquent in council. Like Washington he was a
silent member. Adams and Jefferson both testified
to that. He was also, and perhaps unlike Washington in that, a sleepy member. Chief Justice
White used to nod on the bench, but lawyers were
no less wary of him on that account. It was said
that one might as safely pit a weak argument
against that Chief Justice's nap as to attempt to
enter a strange house over the form of a sleeping
blood-hound.

In another place it has been said of Franklin
that it is easier to state what he did not do in
Congress than what he did. He seems to have been
the type of member who depended on intimate
contact with individuals or, when before an as-

sembly, on persuasion by anecdote rather than by eloquence. In this connection he summed his own virtues: "I was but a bad speaker . . . yet I generally carried my point."

· This is made easily believable, if corroboration of so modest a claim were required, by an incident in the "old congress" when the confederation of the states was strenuously opposed by the states of lesser population and smaller areas for fear they would be swallowed up by the larger and more populous ones. The discussion was led into disagreeable if not quite dangerous ways, with hard words and possible hard feelings, when Franklin benignantly rose to the occasion, not with a speech but with one of his easing little apologues by means of which he seems to have generally, and in this case certainly, to have carried his point.

"At the time of the union of England and Scotland," observed the Doctor, "the Duke of Argyle was most violently opposed to that measure, and among other things predicted, that as the whale had swallowed Jonah, so Scotland would be swallowed by England. However, when Lord Bute came into the Government, he soon brought into the administration so many of his [Scot] countrymen, that it was found in the event that Jonah swallowed the whale." The ensuing laugh eased the situation and the article of difficulty was passed.

So, if not an eloquent, he seems not to have been a silent member of the public assemblies. Nor could his pen have been mightier than such an amiable facile tongue, though he was named with John Adams, Thomas Jefferson, Robert Livingston and Roger Sherman, on the committee to draft the Declaration of Independence. Why he did not actually write that paper has already been suggested. He told Jefferson, however, that he had long since decided not to allow himself to be put in a position wherein anything he had written would be subject to the editing of others.

When the adoption of that instrument definitely brought the Revolution into the open, and put the colonies frankly at war with England, Franklin was immediately chosen to join Silas Deane (he was later superseded by John Adams) and Arthur Lee in Paris. He remained there nine years. Toward the end of 1779 he was made the sole plenipotentiary, and so carried on until he returned home in 1785.

The first three years in France were among the most annoying Franklin ever experienced. He found himself on a commission without a head, yet

treated as its head by all the French from the King
and his Prime Minister, Vergennes, to the crowds
who hailed him whenever he appeared in public.
To the jealousy which this engendered, were added
the bickering and scandal-mongering which passed
between the other commissioners, between them and
Congress, and between them and other American
agents to other European countries to which they
were unwelcome for fear of the offense their
presence would give England, with the result that
they stayed in Paris. The French capital at that
time was a battle-field on which high American
reputations were freely pummeled. Franklin did
not escape. Some of the issues were never quite
clear, and they have not yet been definitely settled.

The most compromising accusations against
Franklin were that he kept on too friendly a basis
with the French and that he allowed his official
papers to get into somewhat of a muddle. He did
not find the latter accusation worth discussing or
denying. As for the former, he proudly admitted
that he admired the French, and cultivated their
friendship as the best and easiest way to secure
their moral and material aid in the war. Friendly
and delightful as he found all his associations with
the French, official and personal, his life among

the Americans in Paris was a veritable hornet's nest. Franklin seemed not at home in a quarrel. He philosophically remained aloof in so far as he could and continued to use his French affiliations for his country's needs.

In spite of the scandals and the discord among his fellow countrymen in Paris, money and supplies went thence to the American colonies and eventually France recognized our independence. If all this advantage is not directly and wholly attributable to Franklin, certainly American interests derived inestimable advantage from the confidence and esteem in which the French of all classes held him. He was the best possible representative the revolutionists could have had in that position.

One thing never heard of the Doctor in the midst of these or any other trials is that he lost his temper. Jefferson, in his *Autobiography,* provided another instance of how Franklin employed anecdote as an escape valve for his emotions. It was when he and Franklin were in France together and the posts brought word from home of the breakdown of government by committee, because Congress split at a moment when it should have given the envoy in France its united support. He sets out how Franklin ignored the exasperation of the situation in telling a story which illustrated the unfailing disposition of human kind to disagree:

"He mentioned the Eddystone lighthouse, in the British channel, as being built on a rock, in the mid-channel, totally inaccessible in winter, from the boisterous character of the sea, in that season; that, therefore, for the two keepers employed to keep up the lights, all provisions for the winter were necessarily carried to them in the autumn, as they could never be visited again till the return of the milder season; that, on the first practicable day in the spring, a boat put off to them with fresh supplies. The boatman met at the door one of the keepers, and accosted him with a 'How goes it, friend? Very well. How is your companion? I do not know. Don't know? Is not he here? I can't tell. Have you not seen him to-day? No. When did you see him? Not since last fall. You have killed him? Not I, indeed.' They were about to lay hold of him as having certainly murdered his companion; but he desired them to go up stairs and examine for themselves. They went up, and there found the other keeper. They had quarrelled, it seems, soon after being left there, had divided into two parties, assigned the cares below to one, and those above to the other, and had never spoken to, or seen, one another since."

BENJAMIN FRANKLIN

There is no fact, in connection with these trying days in France, that need be withheld of the good Doctor. The nearest thing to an untruth of him was smuggled in an intended compliment. When, after the signing of the French treaty, Franklin was invited to Court, much was made of the fact that he appeared before the King without the wig prescribed by Court etiquette, his own white hair flowing loose over his shoulders. Even the French were delighted with this expression of republicanism. The facts exonerate the Doctor of intending unconventionality.

He had ordered a wig, and a *perruquier* brought it to his house in Passy the morning of the royal levee. The artist tried in vain, however, to get it to fit on the Doctor's head, and is represented as having dashed it angrily to the floor.

"Is the wig too small?" asked the placid Doctor.

"No, *Monsieur*," roared the hair-dresser, "your head is too big."

Not bad, even though it were fiction instead of the truth, neatly to point the fact that the old gentleman's philosophical head was too big for the superficialities of court dress.

It was at the signing of the treaty by which the French acknowledged our independence of England and became our ally, that dress really mattered to Franklin. It provided precisely the occasion for which he had been saving that suit of spotted Manchester velvet. The wig did not matter much to him now, but the coat did. Having stood in it for an hour to receive the abuse of the English Attorney General before the entire Privy Council, word of his wearing it the second time, with all the details of the circumstances, were encouraged to cross the English Channel, and thence find their way into print and parley.

Indeed, how little he wigged or thought of wigging, came out in a letter to Mrs. Thompson, an English friend of earlier days in England, to whom he sketched his own portrait:

"I know you wish you could see me; but, as you cannot, I will describe myself to you. Figure me in your mind as jolly as formerly, and as strong and hearty, only a few years older; very plainly dressed, wearing my thin grey straight hair, that peeps out under my only *coiffure,* a fine fur cap, which comes down my forehead almost to my spectacles. Think how this must appear among the powdered heads of Paris! I wish every gentleman and lady in France would only be so obliging as to follow my fashion, comb their own heads as I do mine, dismiss their *friseurs,* and pay me half the money they paid to them. You see, the gentry might well afford to do this, and I could then enlist these *friseurs,* who are at least one hundred thousand, and with the money I would maintain them, make a visit with them to England, and dress the heads of your ministers and privy councillors; which I conceive to be at present *un peu dérangées.*"

He was left alone, in control of the mission in France, in his seventy-fourth year. If, thereafter, he did no single thing that stands out as do his achievements in England, the old gentleman was iron for endurance and steel for sharpness. In addition to concluding a liberal treaty with Prussia and adroitly preventing France from being offended by the treaty concluded with England recognizing our independence, his last six years in Paris were momentous with minutiæ.

He was not merely busy, he was busy with the affairs of every one connected with the Revolution who was off the American continent and beyond the immediate reach of Washington himself. If by natural bent he earlier had been a jack-of-all-trades in science, now he was forced to become a jack-of-all-trades in a position which was supposed to be merely diplomatic.

John Paul Jones, and others operating at sea under the new transatlantic flag, based their naval operations in French ports and reported to Franklin. He had to act as a court of admiralty in disposing of prizes and their cargoes, in adjusting disputes between commanders and their crews, and in attending to the fate of mutineers and to the repairing and refitting of ships. A skipper ran his ship into a West Indian port, for repairs and supplies, and drew on Franklin for the expense. John Jay was sent to Spain to arrange funds to advance the war, but the dons kept their pockets buttoned, and he sent to Franklin for funds to support his mission there. These are samples of repeated instances. The Doctor had to pay without total regard always as to the merits of the claims, lest our capacity to pay be doubted. He not only had to pay, he had also to find the funds with which to pay. Congress sent no funds to support even his own mission; he was expected to find that, too.

He borrowed vast sums from the French to carry on operations in every direction, and then borrowed more from the same source with which to pay them interest on the earlier loans. He negotiated with the English for the exchange of prisoners and for peace. He seems ever to have been on the alert for a trap of some kind, and sometimes found it. He held his commission of Congress, but sometimes independently of him the different states were trying to make other loans at the same sources. Every American with a grievance, and beyond the American continent, in either hemisphere, brought or sent his troubles to the old gentleman at Passy.

He was not merely ambassador, but as well a kind of extra-territorial Secretary of the Navy, Secretary of the Treasury, Secretary of Commerce, Admiralty Judge and Consul General. There indeed were starch and spine, sustaining spirit and energy, behind the little man of curves and smiles, and of graciousness and good nature.

Little wonder then that when he left France he was given a royal progress to the sea-coast. Little wonder that, on reaching home, he was welcomed with "delirious enthusiasm."

He was seventy-nine years old. But his public service was not yet over. Proud Pennsylvania elected, and twice reelected him the President of its supreme Executive Council, in effect its Governor, and in 1787 sent him as her delegate into the convention gathered to frame the Constitution. There, too infirm to stand on his feet and address his colleagues, he wrote out his speeches and they were read to the assembly by a colleague. The speeches of the other delegates were extemporaneous, and were delivered without a stenographic report, so that, curiously, Madison's great feat, of writing the history of that great Convention, was done from his own notes, except for the precise words of the speeches of Franklin. Without his precise words there would be reason to believe that Poor Richard was a philosopher rather than a statesman. But, with them, happily, survives the written evidence of how he was both, and one more indication of how he merited his place in the front rank of the patriot fathers.

The Constitution bears one deep and particular impression of Franklin's practical mind. One of the great contests was between the small states and the large states as to representation in the Congress. It was Franklin who proposed that representation in the Lower House should be made on the basis of proportional population, and that in the Senate each state, regardless of its size and population, should have two representatives, but that all questions of appropriating money must arise in the Lower House, the Senate being privileged to amend or concur. This solution satisfied every one, and it has become one of the most important principles in the Constitution, and one least likely to be changed.

As with other delegates, some of his proposals were rejected, and he disapproved of some that were accepted. But at the end, in urging unanimous subscription to the document, he was able to say:

"I confess that I do not entirely approve of this Constitution; but, sir, I am not sure I shall never approve of it; for, having lived long, I have experienced many instances of being obliged, by better information or fuller consideration, to change my opinions even on important subjects, which I once thought right, but found to be otherwise. . . . Most men, indeed, as well as most sects in religion, think themselves in possession of all the truth, and where others differ from them, it is so far error.

"Steele, a protestant, in a dedication, tells the Pope, that the only difference between our two churches in their opinions of the certainty of their doctrine, is, the Romish Church is *infallible,* and the Church of England is *never in the wrong.* But though many Persons think almost as highly of their own infallibility as of that of their Sect, few express it so naturally as a certain French Lady, who, in a little dispute with her sister, said, 'But I meet with nobody but myself that is *always* in the right.' "

Yet this mind capable of governing the largest of the original states and of taking his place among the most constructive contributors to the nation's charter, and of wrestling successfully with the united statesmen of England and France, was also open to a continuous flow of minor ideas and experiments. In addition to citations of this already made, there is that one in which Bruce draws an amusing picture of him in his last years as he sat in his library in Philadelphia, "surrounded by various objects conceived by his own ingenuity. The seat of his chair became a stepladder, when reversed, and to its arm was fastened a fan which he could work with a slight motion of his foot. Against his bookcase rested 'the long arm' with which he lifted down the books from its upper shelves. The hours, minutes and seconds were told for him by a clock, of his own invention, with only three wheels and two pinions, in which James Ferguson, mathematician as he was, had to confess that he experienced difficulty in making improvements. The very bifocal glasses, now in such general use, that he wore were a triumph of his own quick wit." Franklin, as long as he lived, inquisitive and acquisitive, seemed never to nod, unless, as Adams noted, when forced to listen to congressional oratory.

III

PATRICK HENRY

PATRICK HENRY left just one important paper in his own handwriting for his biographers, from which it may be inferred that he had no high hopes from the group whom a latter phrase-maker called "the body snatchers of literature."

Chief Justice Marshall said: "I hope to God they will let me alone till I am dead!" Henry probably hoped they would let him alone after he was dead. Well he might. Fame seized him early in life and laureled him early in death. Yet it took the biographical embalmers over a century to lay him out properly.

From a century and a quarter of oratory Washington emerges the Sword of the Revolution, Jefferson the Pen of the Revolution and Henry the Tongue of the Revolution. To justify this flaming epitaph on Henry, tradition has bequeathed to us its fallible memory of just two of his speeches. Both of them are known by their final phrases to every generation of schoolboys since his death.

One of them was made in the House of Burgesses at Williamsburg in 1765, and was remembered for his dramatically interrupted recital of certain tyrants and their fates. When he mentioned the reigning monarch, King George III, the cry of "Treason" rose about him, and popular history has since adopted a version which credits Henry with the prompt retort: "If that be treason, make the most of it," and thereby, perhaps, unconsciously, he put one foot upon his pedestal.

It is an uncomfortable metaphor to use in this connection, as it leaves the good man in a rather strained position for a matter of another decade. For only after ten years, this time in the convention which was sitting in St. John's Church, in the little city of Richmond, did he draw up his other foot, as he perorated with his challenging finale: "Give me Liberty, or give me Death!" There in two phrases are the popular supports of the fame of one of the most celebrated characters of the formative period of this country.

Eighteen years after Henry's death, in 1817, William Wirt, a political protégé of Thomas Jefferson, prepared a biography of the great orator. He appealed to Jefferson for his recollections of Henry. Jefferson gave them in a memorandum of about thirty-five hundred words. He was a careful man, leaving behind him only the papers by which he wished to be judged; and this memorandum was not among them. But it survived and appeared later to plague his memory. If Wirt had accepted it on its face value it would have blasted Henry's reputation and left him a political and ethical bankrupt.

It makes the liveliest kind of reading. It "whittles away Henry's good name on small matters, leaving chips all about him as to" his rapacity for fees; his parsimony; his lack of accuracy or logic; his failure as draughtsman of the Petition to the King; his connection with the Yazoo speculation; his acknowledged brilliancy in swaying the passions of his hearers with his oratory, but its inefficiency in swaying the Congress of cool-headed, reflecting, judicious men which reduced him to an uncomfortable silence there. But in the final paragraph Jefferson sought artfully to pay off other scores as well:

"Hamilton became now his idol, and, abandoning the republican advocates of the constitution, the federal government on federal principles became his political creed. Gen[l] Washington flattered him by an appointment to a mission to Spain, which he declined; & by proposing to him the office of Secretary of State, on the most earnest solicitation of Gen[l] Henry Lee, who pledged himself that Henry should not accept it; for Gen[l] Washington knew that he was entirely unqualified for it, & moreover that his self-esteem had never suffered him to act as second to any man on earth. I had this fact from information, but that of the mission to Spain is of my own knolege because after my retiring from the office of Sec[y] of State Gen[l] Washington passed the papers to mr Henry through my hands. mr Henry's apostacy sunk him to nothing in the estimation of his country. he lost at once all that influence which federalism had hoped, by cajoling him, to transfer with him to itself and a man who thro a long & active life had been the idol of his country beyond any one that ever lived, descended to the grave with less than it's indifference, and verified the saying of the philosopher, that no man must be called happy till he is dead."

In spite of Jefferson's prompting, Wirt, due no doubt to an overwhelming admiration for Henry, as well as a judicious appreciation of Jefferson's motives and perspective, took this epitaph with several grains of salt. Since then it has been contradicted effectively by documentations, and the shadow that it was meant to cast on Henry and others is not there.

Significant criticism of Henry did not again show its head until Edward A. Pollard, at once the ablest defender of the Confederacy and the most ruthless critic of Jefferson Davis, fired a broadside at the Henry pedestal in a magazine called *The Galaxy*, for September, 1870. He questioned whether Henry had uttered the historic words put into his mouth and would have reduced him from the status of an orator "to the class distinctly known as stump speakers," though as "an eminent representative of that class," and concluded from his own summary of Henry's inconsistencies that "he must have lacked alike, the consistency of intellectual purpose and the integrity of moral principle to constitute him a great orator."

These reflections on Henry's character, like the others, are adequately repudiated and disproved by the three major biographies of Moses Coit Tyler, his own grandson William Wirt Henry, and George Morgan. The revolutionary patriot emerged at full length, erect and secure, in full possession of his character, one of the fine figures of the epic era of our national birth pangs.

Few patriots, however, have attained permanent celebrity by so little performance. The private lives of few public men have been reconstructed from so little material. Of his own words there are fewer than of any contemporary of his distinction. If ever he wrote his speeches not one survives in his own hand. The only one assuming to be given in his words (other than those delivered in the British Debts case and in the Virginia Convention of 1788, convened to consider the question of the adoption of the United States Constitution), that delivered in St. John's Church, seems first to have been put into print by Wirt, forty years after its delivery, but without indication of source; and, so far as there is authentic evidence, the speech, as it is known, is no more than a version supplied from memory only, years after, by one of those present when Henry spoke. Compared to the surviving letters written by Washington, the two Presidents Adams, Hamilton or Franklin, Jefferson or Madison, those of Patrick Henry are numerically negligible. Nearly all we have of what he may have said is out of other men's mouths.

The testimony of his contemporaries in public life conceded his preeminence as an orator. His entire greatness in this particular seems to have been seriously questioned only by Jefferson, by Pollard, by General Posey and by Doctor Archibold Alexander, a Princeton dominie, who heard Henry in 1794. Among all who did hear him Jefferson may be accepted as a partial witness. But Alexander, whom Henry affected as long as he listened, could counteract such effects the moment he had time for reflection. He supported this view by citing General Posey, of Revolutionary fame:

"He [General Posey] was in attendance at the debates of that Convention in which there were so many displays of deliberative eloquence. He assured me, that after hearing Patrick Henry's most celebrated speech in that body, he felt himself as fully persuaded that the Constitution as adopted would be our ruin, as of his own existence. Yet subsequent reflection restored his former judgment, and his well considered opinion resumed its place."

"Your passions are no longer your own when he addresses them," said George Mason, which would seem to confirm the claim that Henry's eloquence reached the emotions and not the intellect, and lost its grip when thoughtful men regained control of

themselves. But Mason made this statement
incident to a thoughtful and sincere tribute to
Henry, in which he also said:

"He is by far the most powerful speaker I have
ever heard. . . . But his eloquence is the smallest
part of his merit. He is, in my opinion, the first
man upon this Continent, as well in abilities as
public virtues." And General Knox feared "that
overwhelming torrent, Patrick Henry."

A recent find, however, appears to deal a blow
at the "remembered," in distinction to the "docu-
mented," history of the exact words of one of
Henry's two most famous periods. For over one
hundred years, on what represents itself as tradition, Henry has been credited with that ringing
retort, "If that be treason, make the most of it!"
The phrase got into print first in John Burk's
History of Virginia, published in 1805. It might
have been based on a letter written thirty days
after Henry's speech, for such a letter at the time
of Burk's writing and until quite recently, has
been the earliest known record of that utterance.
Wirt followed Burk, supporting him with this
from Jefferson:

"I well remember the cry of treason, the pause
of Mr. Henry at the name of George III, and the
presence of mind with which he closed his sentence."

PATRIOTS OFF THEIR PEDESTALS

All the while, however, and ever since, there has been another eye-witness, one who daily wrote what he heard and saw on each day, a Frenchman traveling in America in 1765. It is not known why he came to America, but he was a close observer, and the fidelity of his observations on nature and geography, which may be confirmed to-day, argue for the probability of his accuracy. His *Journal* came to light in Paris in 1920, in the archives of the *Service Hydrographique de la Marine,* and a photostatic copy of it has recently been placed in the Library of Congress. He used English, but with a curious arbitrary way of capitalizing the letters C, D and E in the middle of sentences. Under the date of May thirtieth, he wrote:

"Set out Early from halfway house in the Chair and broke fast at York, arrived at williamsburg at 12, where I saw three Negroes hanging at the galous for haveing robed Mr. Waltho of 300 ps. I went immediately to the Assembly which was seting, where I was entertained with very strong Debates Concerning Dutys that the parlement wants to lay on the American colonys, which they Call or Stile stamp Dutys. Shortly after I Came in one of the members stood up and said he had read that in former times tarquin and Julus had their Brutus, Charles had his Cromwell, and he Did not Doubt but that some good american would stand up, in favour of his Country, but (says he) in a more moderate manner, and was going to Continue, when the speaker of the house rose and Said, he, the last that stood up had spoke traison, and was sorey to see that not one of the member of the house was loyal Enough to stop him, before he had gone so far. upon which the Same member stood up again (his name is henery) and said that if he had afronted the speaker, or the house, he was ready to ask pardon, and he would shew his loyalty to his majesty King G. the third, at the Expence of the last Drop of his blood, but what he had said must be atributed to the Interest of his Countrys Dying liberty which he had at heart, and the heat of passion might have lead him to have said more than he intended, but, again, if he said anything wrong, he beged the speaker and the houses pardon. some other Members stood up and backed him, on which the afaire was droped."

Here is the only surviving evidence of the famous happening written on the day of its happening. Did the Frenchman record incorrectly, or was the celebrated phrase a fiction? Did the contemporaries retell the story of "traison" over so many times, each embellishing a bit, over so many years, that with handling it grew polished, and with repetition it became accepted? Legends reduplicated and standardized make it the easier for realism to weaken and to accept them in their unreal form. It is said that the Duke of Wellington, finally, in his old age, admitted, to save trouble, that he had, at Waterloo, really said, "Up, guards, and at 'em!" Could it have been that even Mr. Henry would, or did, succumb similarly?

The "afaire" may have been "droped," but not its effect. In spite of the possible disillusionment in the matter of a single phrase, it may be significant of the effect produced by Mr. "henery," that the same Journal records:

"The Kings Berth Night which was on the tuesday follow'g, was given by the lieutanant governor mr. farquier. I went there in Expectation of seeing a great Deal of Company, but was Dissapointed for there was not more than a Dozen of people. I came away before super."

Francis Fauquier was the most popular governor that the Crown sent to Virginia. The affront of the absence of the Burgesses and citizens was not intended by them as an affront to him, but for the King. The Revolution was on, and something in Henry's treasonable utterance had helped it at this time in this particular expression.

Henry's activities were about equally divided between a public career in the House of Burgesses, in the Congress, and as Governor of Virginia, and a private career as a lawyer. He was highly successful when arguing in court, and, when he died, he was considered, by the measure of his own day, as rich. He was an up-country man as distinguished from a tidewater man. He seemed all his life to have been nearer the soil than the city.

It may be consoling to the ambition of other boys to know that this man, when a boy, was a truant from school; studied nature and the laws of nature lying on his back on a shady bank watching the trees and the sky and the creatures; that when the canoe, in which he and his cronies had their sport, overturned in the water, it generally happened that the others had their clothes on and he had none; that he mimicked his elders, gunned and fished and swam, and did no work that he had not to do.

When he applied for a license to practise law he had already made an impression by his "genius," and, though he admitted that he had been studying only six weeks, he was nevertheless admitted to the bar on his mere promise to study. He never became a bookish man. Yet he tried. He borrowed books frequently, kept them by the year, and returned them with the confession that he had been unable to read them. When cornered by necessity, in his practise, he would devour a book, cram himself with its contents at one sitting, and use the material brilliantly in the cause he was pleading.

In the company of the aristocratic celebrities among whom he found himself in public life, by the side of Washington, Jefferson, Madison, the Pages and Carters and Lees, it would seem that, at first, in the simplicity of his dress and the unconventionality of his manner, Henry presented some suggestion of the artless Lincoln.

If early he was remembered to have worn coarse apparel, with grease smearing his leather breeches, and otherwise to have been careless in his dress, he made an effort to correct this when later he emerged into public life. He sensed the disparity between himself and those about him, for, in the House of Burgesses at Williamsburg, he dressed his head in "a caul-bare wig" and he graduated into a "peach blossom colored coat." Later he receded into a suit of black with a white neckscarf. In spite of his efforts at conservatism, the rhetorical flame of his oratory got nevertheless into his garments, for in the winter sessions of the Legislature, he habitually appeared wrapped in "a red velvet mantle." Henry's friends, from whom such details are picked up, reveal him, for all his patriotic honesty and his forensic power, natively a bit theatrical, a scrap of an actor.

Like his speeches, the few anecdotes that have been told of him are merely traditional, remembered versions, embellished on their way from lip to lip and from pen to pen, "tinctured by the medium through which they have passed." They are such stories as might be told of many shrewd trial lawyers. One of them at least betrays overshrewd equivocation. They are more certainly amusing than authentic, and may be taken or left as fables of a fame which, authentic in its larger sense, is so much of a myth in many of its details.

In offering the divided shoat story, Morgan swallows hard on its credibility: "Since Henry undoubtedly had a 'tendency to grace,' it is hard to believe the traditional shoat story heard in the Lynchburg region, where he is still spoken of as 'the Governor.' It is told about in this style: 'A man stole a hog, dressed it, and went to the Governor to defend him. The Governor said:

" ' "Did you walk away with that shoat?"

" ' "Yessir."

" ' "Have you got the carcass?"

" ' "Yessir."

" ' "You go home, you wretch; cut the pig lengthwise in half, and hang as much of it in my smoke-house as in yours."

" 'At Court the Governor said:

" ' "Your Honor, this man has no more of that shoat than I have. If necessary, I'd kiss the Bible on this."

" 'The man was cleared.' "

No apology is needed for an anecdote rehearsed by Henry Clay, in a speech delivered in 1811 in this fashion: "He [Patrick Henry] mistook, in one instance, the side of the cause in which he was retained, and addressed the court and jury in a very masterly and convincing speech, in behalf of his antagonist. His distracted client came up to him, while he was thus employed, and, interrupting, bitterly exclaimed:

" 'You have undone me! You have ruined me!'

" 'Never mind—give yourself no concern,' said the adroit advocate, and turning to the court and jury, continued his argument, by observing,

" 'May it please your honors, and you gentlemen of the jury, I have been stating to you what I presume my adversary may urge on his side. I will now show how fallacious his reasonings, and how groundless his pretensions are.'

"The skillful orator proceeded, satisfactorily refuted every argument he had advanced, and gained his cause!"

Most popular of all the tales of Henry is that of his retaliation on Francis Corbin, who sought to cross rapiers with the older man. Young Corbin had spent the greater part of the Revolutionary war period in England, "where as a college student and courtier he had gathered polish." He chose the floor of the House for the scene of his attack, and based it on Henry's assurance, in regard to amendments under discussion, that "he was ready and willing, at all times and on all occasions, to bow with the utmost deference to the majesty of the people."

Corbin, in discussing Henry's attitude, punctuated each period with sarcastic reference to his "bow to the majesty of the people," and himself bowing with a grave courtier-like sweep. Thirteen times he repeated the phrase and the bow. Wirt, in his account, said:

"The young gentleman, having finished his

philippic, very much at least to his own satisfaction, took his seat with the gayest expression of triumph on his countenance. . . . Mr. Henry raised himself up, heavily, and with affected awkwardness——

" 'Mr. Speaker,' said he, 'I am a plain man, and have been educated altogether in Virginia. My whole life has been spent among planters, and other plain men of similar education, who have never had that polish which a court alone can give, and which the gentleman over the way has so happily acquired; indeed, sir, the gentleman's employments and mine (in common with the great mass of his countrymen) have been as widely different as our fortunes; for while that gentleman was availing himself of the opportunity which a splendid fortune afforded him, of acquiring a foreign education, mixing among the great, attending levees and courts, basking in the beams of royal favour at St. James', and exchanging courtesies with crowned heads, I was engaged in the arduous toils of the Revolution; and was probably as far from thinking of acquiring those polite accomplishments which the gentleman has so successfully cultivated, as that gentleman then was from sharing in the toils and dangers in which his unpolished countrymen were engaged. I will not, therefore, presume to vie with the gentleman in those courtly accomplishments, of which he has just given the House so agreeable a specimen; yet such a bow as I can make, shall be ever at the service of the people.'——

"Herewith, although there was no man who could make a more graceful bow than Mr. Henry, he made one so ludicrously awkward and clownish, as took the house by surprise, and put them in a roar of laughter.

" 'The gentleman, I hope, will commiserate the disadvantages of education under which I have laboured, and will be pleased to remember, that I have never been a favourite with that monarch, whose gracious smile he has had the happiness to enjoy.'

"He pursued this contrast of situations and engagements, for fifteen or twenty minutes, without a smile, and without the smallest token of resentment, either in countenance, expression or manner.

" 'You could have sworn,' says a correspondent, 'that he thought himself making his apology for his own awkwardness, before a full drawing-room at St. James'. I believe there was not a person that heard him, the sufferer himself excepted, who did not feel every risible nerve affected. His adversary meantime hung down his head, and, sinking lower and lower, until he was almost concealed behind the interposing forms, submitted to the discipline as quietly as a Russian malefactor, who had been beaten with the knout, till all sense of feeling was lost.' "

If the effect of his oratory was Homeric while he held his hearers' passions in its spell, and sometimes waned when it released the emotions, he did nothing else so genuinely and lastingly affecting as his final simple gesture. It might have been an episode out of a Greek tragedy.

He lay on his death-bed in his sixty-third year. His physician handed him a dose of liquid mercury, and, questioned, admitted that without it he could live only a short time; but that, if he took it, it would give him immediate relief or prove immediately fatal. The dying man did not hesitate. Drawing over his eyes a silk cap he was accustomed to wear, he received the vial in his hand, prayed in clear words for a moment, and swallowed the drug. He took the chance heroically, and heroically lost.

IV

ALEXANDER HAMILTON

"To CONFESS my weakness, Ned, my ambition is prevalent, so that I contemn the grovelling condition of a clerk, or the like, and would willingly risk my life, though not my character to exalt my station. I am confident, Ned, that my youth excludes me from any hope of immediate preferment, nor do I desire it; but I mean to prepare the way for futurity. I'm no philosopher, you see, and may be justly said to build castles in the air; my folly makes me ashamed, and beg you'll conceal it; yet, Neddy, we have seen such schemes successful, when the projector is constant. I will conclude by saying I wish there was a war."

So, in 1769, toward the end of his thirteenth year, young Alexander Hamilton wrote a British colonial friend in the island of Nevis of the British West Indies, where he himself was born and lived at the time. For all its oldish manner, like other letters of the period, it is breezily youthful, with its

97

high spirits and high ambition; and he remained youthful at heart all his days. His spirits soared to the end of his life. As for his precocious ambitions, he realized surprisingly well and surprisingly early on them. And, too, he soon had his war.

He had shaken off the islands within three years, and found himself in New York. After another three years, he having not yet completed his own seventeenth, he attracted attention as a patriotic orator and disputant, and when only twenty years old he was called by General Washington to become one of his aides-de-camp with the rank of Lieutenant Colonel.

The salient features of his subsequent life, for which he is best known, are that he was a member of the convention that framed the Constitution, the chief contributor to *The Federalist* in defense of the Constitution, Secretary of the Treasury in President Washington's Cabinet, founder of the financial system of the Republic, the object of Jefferson's political antagonism and hatred, father of the Federal Party which he lived to see dead on his hands, and that in his forty-eighth year, he fell in a duel with Aaron Burr.

Whatever the type of his ambition may have been when as a boy he shot up in life, with years and attainment he shed any disposition to succeed for any personal, selfish or mean ambition. His object was not personal glory. Had this not been so he would not, as he so often did, have sacrificed his popularity to his principles and his opinions.

It was not alone, however, because Hamilton was spurred by a youthful ambition or that he was a prodigy of youthful attainment, that the young West Indian raised himself to the stars. By make-up he was a genius with a passion for achievement. He made himself a scholar of profound and solid attainment. Moreover, he made himself master in every arena he entered, and Lodge points out, "however he may have erred in moments of passion, he never failed." Marshall ranked him "second to Washington," and Talleyrand said: "I consider Napoleon, Fox and Hamilton as the three greatest men of our epoch, and if I had to choose among them, I would without hesitating give the first place to Hamilton."

On his pedestal he is orator, soldier, lawyer, banker, writer and statesman, but his life was given glamour and romance by the enemies he made. He made enemies, because, said Sumner, "His fearless-ness, openness and directness turned rivals into enemies, irritated smaller men, and aroused their malicious desire to pull him down. At the same time by the mass he was not understood, and in them he inspired a vague sense of alienation and distrust." He held popular opinion of no value and failed to recognize that it nevertheless had power.

Hamilton seemed all his life to have been imagined to dwell in a glass house. It may of course be expected that the windows of a man's public life shall be without shades or blinds and that its doors shall swing both ways and without hindrance. But Hamilton's political enemies seemed not to be willing to admit that a man should be granted the proprietorship of his unofficial life, and that he be privileged to work out the humanities with his own conscience.

The singular thing, however, about the efforts of his enemies to discredit him, and one of the most interesting features of the life of this brilliant character, to whom it appears to have been unique, is that the arrows of defamation seemed never to reach a vulnerable point. However they were directed, an invisible hand seemed to change their course and their effect. Aimed at his vitals, they lodged in his bonnet, where fate made of them a kind of decoration. His enemies illustrated Franklin's metaphor, for their own faces showed that they spat against the wind. John Adams, James Monroe and Aaron Burr were the unconscious decorators of Hamilton's metaphorical bonnet.

Adams referred to Hamilton as "the bastard brat of a Scotch peddler." The sneer suggests far more than the facts sustain. Hamilton's mother was of good family and was first married to a Dane named Levine. He was much older than she was, and was so cruel in his treatment of her that she was obliged to leave him and return to her mother's house. The disorderly condition of the provincial courts, in the islands, prevented her from getting a divorce from the man who ruined her life, but they did not prevent Levine from divorcing her. It was several years after she had left this man that she met James Hamilton and fell in love with him, and that they began their life together as husband and wife, a relationship that lasted until her death. Though without formal legal sanction, they do not seem, on account of that relationship, to have incurred any loss of caste in the community where they lived, and it certainly was not regarded as a hindrance to the proud patroon of Albany, General Philip Schuyler, from giving Hamilton his daughter Eliza in marriage, or from fondly doting on his son-in-law all the rest of his life.

Another fame might have clouded before such a slur as that of Adams. ˙Intended to discredit Hamilton, it has become one of his badges. That slur, which Hamilton's fame has eclipsed, has been repeatedly used to illustrate the handicap he bore and to measure the long way he came up in spite of it to the heights where his attainments have secured him.

Another of his life's little ironies was provided by the Reynolds Case. At bottom it is a story reflecting no credit on any one concerned, perhaps least of all on Hamilton himself, except in his brave and masterly handling of the dilemma in which his political enemies thought they had securely trapped him.

While he was Secretary of the Treasury, in Philadelphia, Hamilton's adversaries sought in every way to get evidence of his misuse of both the public funds, and of the information confidential to his office, for speculation. Every open charge and veiled hint had been answered by Hamilton in a manner to leave no doubt of his integrity, when from a most unexpected quarter a real opening to his vitals seemed to have presented itself.

In 1792 the Philadelphia jail held two rascals, one Clingman and one Reynolds, on the charge of "subornation to perjury" in an attempt to obtain fraudulently the payment of a debt due from the United States. Muhlenburg, at the time the Speaker of the House of Representatives, interested himself in behalf of Clingman, whereupon Clingman intimated that his fellow-prisoner, Reynolds, had a certain high officer of the government in his power. The name mentioned was Hamilton.

The Speaker confided the information to Senator James Monroe and Representative Venable, both of Virginia, and the trio visited the prison and heard what Reynolds had to say, and later had an interview with Reynolds' wife.

On the evidence contained in their notes of the conversations with these worthies, and armed with four anonymous, non-significant notes which it was alleged were Hamilton's, the three members of Congress visited the Secretary of the Treasury.

They perhaps believed, and probably hoped, that they had his political ruin in their hands; and Hamilton must have sensed another attack on his integrity at their very appearance at his door, for the three men were his avowed political enemies, leaders among the Jeffersonians who hounded him at every imagined opportunity.

PATRIOTS OFF THEIR PEDESTALS

They presented the notes and memoranda, hinted that Hamilton had been concerned with Reynolds in buying up old claims against the government, and were silent for his answer. Hamilton knew his official integrity was at stake. He knew, too, that he could save it only at the price of taking these men into his confidence, by means of a confession to them of human weakness which had for some time held him subject to Reynolds' blackmail.

He did not hesitate. He told them the whole sordid story of an amour of his with Mrs. Reynolds, conducted in part with the knowledge and consent of her husband; produced letters in evidence; and proved that the money which Reynolds had exacted from him was comparatively inconsiderable and was in no way connected with official funds or information. At the conclusion of the confession the three inquisitors declared that they were satisfied, and retired.

The price in pride which he had paid by thus baring his secret soul to his enemies must have seemed to him, and to them, the limit of what might be expected of the proud young aristocrat. But it was not the limit. Fate had another exaction to make, further toll to take, and he met them with an immeasurably greater heroism.

The next day after the interview, he asked for and received copies of the memoranda and notes, and the three inquisitors agreed to keep the originals from the owners, in order to prevent their misuse or publication. It is a question whether even then Monroe was plotting another attack with the same ammunition. It is at least certain that he again saw Clingman, who declared that Hamilton's explanation had been preconcerted between Hamilton and Reynolds to cover the alleged irregularities, and of such stuff Monroe made another memorandum which, together with all the other papers he had in his possession, he handed to "a respectable character in Virginia," who is believed to have given them, four years later, to Callender who at least became possessed of them at that time and thereupon published them to the world in his history.

Hamilton immediately wrote asking the three men for an explanation. Muhlenburg and Venable repudiated any connection with the publication, and wrote that they had never had copies of the papers and had been entirely satisfied with Hamilton's explanation. Monroe, however, evaded and dodged about, until Hamilton charged him with being malevolent and dishonorable. Then Monroe said he was ready to fight. Hamilton asked him to send a challenge. Monroe declared he had no intention of sending such a missive. Hamilton then took other means, the only other he deemed efficacious, to wipe out the stain upon his public character.

His first confession was made to three men in the privacy of his own library, in a confidence which he had a right to believe inviolable. Now the challenge to his official integrity was publicly made, the indictment was before the whole world, the case was in the hands of history. Perhaps Monroe and "the respectable character in Virginia" believed that Hamilton would not dare to make the further sacrifice necessary to defend himself. They may have thought him securely trapped and unwilling and unable to make to the world the confession that he wrung from himself and laid before them in a confidence which he believed had the secrecy of the confessional. They did not imagine him capable of publicly humiliating himself, or openly admitting his private frailty to his wife, to her family, to all the social and political world into which he had raised himself and of which he was a leader, to his own generation and to posterity. It showed by how much they were mistaken in Hamilton.

He retired once more to his library, this time alone, and there set down in writing the whole sordid business. Then he published it, supported by all the documents, in the ever since famous *Reynolds Pamphlet*.

It was one of the most astonishing acts of personal humiliation for the sake of public vindication that history records. He risked the sacrifice of the people's regard for him personally to support his principle that the people must not lose confidence in their public servants.

The private peccadillo was somehow obscured, if not quite erased, by the heroic decision by which he again vindicated and saved his official honor. Again fate betrayed the betrayers. Again the arrow aimed at his vitals lodged in his bonnet where it remained a badge of heroism.

Hamilton risked all. His loss was not in the loyalty of those who mattered. His wife was unshaken in her constancy, and fought on, until death silenced her in her ninety-seventh year, fifty years after his death, ever the champion of the man she loved and who she knew truly loved her. It is not known that Hamilton lost a friend. His father-in-law, General Schuyler, his family, private friends and public followers were unremittingly loyal.

Perhaps the most touching and cherished evidence of sympathy came from a most unexpected source. Hamilton's enemies, during his lifetime and since, have taken pains to represent him as estranged from Washington from the time that, in a moment of youthful conceit, he withdrew himself from the General's staff. Washington's position was now such that he had to exercise great care in committing himself to writing in so delicate a situation, for he knew that eventually every line he wrote would find its way into print and be subjected to each reader's private interpretation. As soon as Hamilton's self-vindication, contained in the astonishing confession, reached Mount Vernon, the General after a long silence which might have suggested the abandonment of their correspondence, immediately wrote his favorite of "his sincere regard and friendship," and that Hamilton "would be persuaded, that with every sentiment of highest regard," he "remained" his "sincere friend," in the following letter:

"Mount Vernon.
"21st August, 1797.

"My dear Sir,—Not for any intrinsic value the thing possesses, but as a token of my sincere regard and friendship for you, and as a remembrance of me; I pray you to accept a Wine cooler for four bottles, which Col¹. Biddle is directed to forward from Philadelphia, (where with other articles it was left) together with this letter, to your address.

"It is one of four, which I imported in the early part of my late Administration of the Government; two only of which were ever used.

"I pray you to present my best wishes, in which Mrs. Washington joins me, to Mrs. Hamilton & the family; and that you would be persuaded, that with every sentiment of the highest regard, I remain your sincere friend, and affectionate Hble. Servant,

Go. Washington."

A part of Eliza Hamilton's fidelity to her husband's memory was her unforgivingness of Monroe. When both were very old, he came to see her in her home in Washington. A nephew, at the time a lad of fifteen years, preserved this account of the interview:

"I had been sent to call upon my Aunt Hamilton one afternoon. I found her in her garden and was there with her talking, when her maid-servant came from the house with a card. It was the card of James Monroe. She read the name, and stood holding the card, much perturbed. Her voice sank, and she spoke very low, as she always did when she was angry.

"'What has that man come to see me for?' escaped from her.

"'Why, Aunt Hamilton,' said I, 'don't you know, it's Mr. Monroe, and he's been President, and he is visiting here now in the neighborhood, and has been very much made of, and invited everywhere, and so—and so I suppose he has come to call and pay his respects to you.'

"After a moment's hesitation, 'I will see him,' she said.

"The maid went back into the house, my aunt followed, walking rapidly, I after her.

"As she entered the parlour, Monroe rose. She stood in the middle of the room facing him. She did not ask him to sit down. He bowed, and addressing her formally, made her a rather set speech—that it was many years since they had met, that the lapse of time brought its softening influences, that they both were nearing the grave, when past differences could be forgiven and forgotten—in short, from his point of view, a very nice, conciliatory, well-turned little speech.

"She answered, still standing, and looking at

him, 'Mr. Monroe, if you have come to tell me that you repent, that you are sorry, *very* sorry, for the misrepresentations and slanders, and the stories that you circulated against my dear husband, if you have come to say this, I understand it. But, otherwise, no lapse of time, no nearness to the grave, makes any difference.'

"She stopped speaking, Monroe turned, took up his hat and left the room."

The third of the conspicuous ironies in Hamilton's life was the incident which terminated it. Hamilton had repeatedly stood between the public and Aaron Burr's aspirations. He had an early and a precise estimate of that character. Rebuffed by the Federalists, which is to say by Hamilton, Burr turned to Jefferson, but there again he found suspicion and dislike. His position in national politics was crumbling. From New England he thought at the moment that he heard whisperings of secession; and he imagined that in such a situation he saw his way upward again to national supremacy by a new route. He sought the governorship of New York as a secure position from which to advantage himself of the northern secession and secure for himself the presidency of a possible northern republic.

Again Hamilton defeated him. Burr's angry disappointment stung him into an act of physical revenge. Unable to stir Hamilton from his public position by the process of politics, Burr resolved to remove him by other means. He deliberately set about picking a quarrel and challenged Hamilton to a duel. In spite of his aversion to the code, Hamilton felt that, in the circumstances, he was obliged to accept the challenge, and he did.

Burr prepared for the duel by pistol practise in his own garden. Hamilton prepared for eventualities by putting his clients' affairs in order, and in writing letters and papers to be opened in case he fell. In one he declared his intention of reserving his first and possibly his second fire. In the same paper, referring to his criticism of Burr, he wrote:

"I certainly have had strong reasons for what I have said, though it is possible that in some particulars I have been influenced by misconstructions or misinformation. It is also my ardent wish that I may have been more mistaken than I think I have been; and that he, by his future conduct, may show himself worthy of all confidence and esteem, and prove an ornament and a blessing to his country." Burr's subsequent career gave his own answer to this strained hope. When they met, Hamilton discharged his pistol into the air, and he fell mortally wounded by Burr's first shot.

Burr may now have thought his path cleared. But he merely killed Hamilton, he did not remove him. The living Hamilton was never more definitely in Burr's path than Hamilton dead. Burr had not realized that Hamilton possessed some of the aspects of a man of destiny.

John Adams's sneer helped to point Hamilton's career as a prodigy of attainment. Monroe's effort to drive Hamilton into disgrace drew from him instead his most heroic gesture. Burr's bullet made of Hamilton a martyr, who, in falling before America's other Arnold, rose in spirit as one of the most romantic figures in our history.

Hamilton's life was pointed with other little ironies and piquant antitheses. One of them confronted him when he felt forced to accept Burr's challenge to a duel. It was not a little difficult for him, not only because his religious and moral principles were opposed to the code, but because, less than three years before, his own oldest boy, Philip, had been taken from him by an antagonist's bullet on "the field of honour." He had told his son to fire his first shot into the air, even as he himself deliberately wasted his first shot when facing Burr.

Another seems to have been produced by the request of President Washington, in accordance with which Hamilton drew up a code of etiquette for the chief executive. It is vain to speculate by how much Jefferson, in his unconventionalities in the White House, was stimulated by antagonism to those rules for his conduct and ceremony prepared by Hamilton; certainly they might have fretted a nature which was so easily irritated by anything else Hamilton did. By the same token, the flaunting of this code of etiquette may have been mischievously designed to irritate the great Federalist.

It is not a little singular, too, that pronounced as was the mutual antipathy between these two political giants, Hamilton found himself forced into a position of responsibility for achieving Jefferson's election to the Presidency. At the end of John Adams's administration, the Federalist party found itself split wide open by a bitter political quarrel between Adams and Hamilton. In this situation the votes of the electoral college were equally divided between Jefferson and Burr, which carried the choice into the House of Representatives. The Federalist members of Congress were eager for the opportunity to overwhelm the powerful leader of the opposition party. Hamilton had suffered severely under Jefferson's attacks, but he knew Burr to be "shallow, dangerous and utterly unscrupulous," and he did not hesitate, as leader of his own party, to use all his influence to save it and the country from the onus of Burr. As a result Burr was defeated and Jefferson was elected President. Incidentally thereby Hamilton committed an act of political self-immolation. It was the end of his Federal party.

Hamilton on his personal side is largely hearsay. There is not a gleam of humor in all his contributions to *The Federalist*. Those papers are as impersonal as uncut marble. There is preserved apparently not a single anecdote of his telling, and none of significance told of him. Yet his sister-in-law, Angelica, enjoyed the "agreable nonsense" which she testified that he knew how to talk; Maclay sat near him at a public dinner and remarked his "very boyish giddy manner"; his doting father-in-law over and over again in his letters referred to "my Hamilton," "our Hamilton," "my beloved Hamilton," and signed himself "most affectionately" or with such phrases as "let the children share with you in that tender affection which I feel with so much force"; and his own letters to his wife and a few intimates display the light touch of one whom humor had not passed by, nor charm, nor spirits, nor the love of living.

This to his affianced a few months before they were married reflects as well as any other written words of Hamilton the grace and charm and tenderness of the boy who grew up but never grew old:

"I have told you and I told you truly that I love you too much. You engross my thoughts too entirely to allow me to think of anything else. You not only employ my mind all day, but you intrude on my sleep. I meet you in every dream, and when I wake I cannot close my eyes again for ruminating on your sweetness. 'T is a pretty story indeed that I am to be thus monopolized by a little *nut brown maid* like you and from a soldier metamorphosed into a puny lover. I believe in my soul that you are an enchantress; but I have tried in vain, if not to break, at least to weaken the charm and you maintain your empire in spite of all my efforts and after every new one I make to draw myself from my allegiance, my partial heart still returns and clings to you with increased attachment. To drop figures, my lovely girl, you become dearer to me every moment."

Everything that is known supports Oliver in his portrait of "the little lion":

ALEXANDER HAMILTON

"There is in all Hamilton's work—writings and speeches—the intense seriousness of youth. The qualities that made him a great statesman were force, lucidity and conviction. His confidence in himself and in his ideas is amazing, amounting almost to fanaticism. . . . If we seek for a complete presentment of the man in what he wrote and spoke we shall not find it. He treats his public ceremoniously and with reserve. An excessive gravity is the rule. Anger is the only passion which is permitted to appear; not a beam of humour or a flash of wit. . . . This also is in accordance with the nature of youth. . . . This serious young statesman we gather to have been remarkable in private life chiefly for his high spirits, his good looks, his bright eyes, and his extraordinary vivacity. He loved the society of his fellow creatures and shone in it. He loved good wine and good company and beautiful things—even clothes and ruffles and fine lace. . . . He belonged to the age of manners, and silk stockings, and handsome shoebuckles. In Bagehot's excellent phrase, he was 'an enjoying English gentleman'; companionable and loyal, gay and sincere, always masterful and nearly always dignified."

V

JOHN ADAMS

WITH an almost comic reticence, it has been said that Mr. Adams's appearance on the scene "generally added to the variety of the entertainment." It is an economy of statement that is almost clarion. It rivals the economy of that artist who was said to have used only three strokes to draw the Archbishop of Canterbury in a wheelbarrow, two for the wheelbarrow and one for the Archbishop.

All Adams's virtues and all his frailties, for not even his enemies attributed vices to him, were positive, turbulent, energetic and fearless. His body may have succumbed to fatigue, but his restless, hungry, insatiable mind knew no repose so long as it inhabited its mortal shell.

Of this, the supporting evidence is all at first hand, bristling and bubbling and spouting out of his own writings. He was in fact peculiarly a man of the pen. He kept a diary, a daily journal, often

118

of extended entries, for forty-one years, and into
it he swept all his experiences and all his thoughts.
This he supplemented with an autobiography. Beyond these self-expressions his numerous letters
were at times long as tracts and pamphlets. And
these are all beside his essays, his public utterances
and his official papers.

Nevertheless, scarcely anything in detail is
known of his youth. He seems to spring to life
with the first lines of his diary, which he began in
his twentieth year. He began it with an earthquake, but forty years later he concluded it with
peace.

That first entry, of November 18, 1755, begins:
"We had a very severe shock of earthquake. It
continued for nearly four minutes. The house
seemed to rock and reel and crack, as if it would
fall in ruins about us."

The entry of September 8, 1796, made in his
sixty-first year, concludes the diary with: "I think
to christen my place by the name of Peacefield, in
commemoration of the peace which I assisted in
making in 1793, of the thirteen years of peace and
neutrality which I contributed to preserve, and of
the constant peace and tranquility which I have
enjoyed in this residence."

PATRIOTS OFF THEIR PEDESTALS

It is not beside the point that the Adams homestead did not fall in ruins under the Massachusetts earthquake, and that he did not name the house at Quincy Peacefield. During the nearly forty-one years of intermittent diary, which he "scribbled" with a fidelity which is astonishing, and on nearly every other sheet to which he put his pen, he wrote and rewrote himself as a sort of human earthquake which threw out verbal lava that did no damage, unless to the dear, vain, jealous patriot himself, and in the end, although he helped prodigiously to give his country peace, he was, consistent to himself, arguing, complaining, speculating, blustering, and genuinely devoted and kindly as long as he held a pen. Jefferson gave Madison, in the course of a correspondence whose confidences drove it into cipher, Franklin's opinion of Adams's character: "Always an honest one, often a great one, but sometimes absolutely mad."

Adams's early energy he worked off with his pen. But the urge to write never left him. Copying sermons and books was his youthful method of study and assimilation. In middle life, to his wife, he confessed in a score of ways what he confessed in these two: "I can't be easy without a pen in my hand," and "I wish I could write you oftener than I do. I wish I could write you a dozen letters a day." Recurrent, too, to friends, such fretting phrases as: "If I had good eyes and fingers, I could write you sheets, if not volumes." The memorable correspondence with Jefferson in the last years of the two Titans so full of affectionate protestations, was evidence that that early urge never left him. He wrote four letters to Jefferson's one. "Neither eyes, fingers or paper held out to despatch all the trifles I wished to write in my last letter"; again, "I will not persecute you so severely in future, if I can help it"; or, "I cannot write the hundredth of what I wish to say." When his fingers at last did give out, his vigorous mind did not, and others took up his pen, and he dictated incredible lengths of letters as long as life lasted.

As for public speaking he used it only when urgently required, and his eloquence was scarcely emotional or rhetorical, but took its persuasion from his great head full of facts, his philosophic mind, and the urge of a patriotism which was irresistible as the tide.

There is a fashion of numbering as well as citing the outstanding facts that made John Adams's career distinguished. His brave undertaking, in the face of an outraged citizenry and regardless of its effect on his own popularity, of the legal defense of the British officers and men responsible for the Boston Massacre, was the first. His proposal of George Washington for the chief command of the colonial army, was the second. This was in Congress sitting in Philadelphia in 1775, and probably nothing in the eulogy of Washington which Adams delivered on that occasion could have equaled the unconscious compliment in the corollary to his entry of that day's doings in his diary: "Mr. Washington who happened to sit near the door, as soon as he heard me allude to him, from his usual modesty, darted into the library room." Adams's speech in advocacy of the adoption of the Declaration of Independence was his third great achievement. His fourth was the results he obtained on his mission to Holland where he secured an early recognition of the national independence of the American colonies and an invaluable supporting loan. The part he took in negotiating the treaty with Great Britain, by which the English finally and formally acknowledged American independence is numbered five in the chronicle. That was in 1783.

He remained abroad as Minister to England until 1788 when he recrossed the ocean and was elected Vice-President and then President. Nothing, however, in his administrations of these offices equaled those earlier achievements, although he will always be held in especial remembrance for the last act of his public career when he selected and appointed John Marshall to be Chief Justice of the Supreme Court of the United States.

Those enumerated contributions of Adams to his country would be incomplete without including himself. He was his own contribution because he was so obviously a self-made man. And as he whacked away at himself, and noted each day's work in his diary, one seems to hear the clang of hammer on rivets, and see the Colossus build. Every great man is in a way, of course, a self-made man, and few of Adams's conspicuous American contemporaries were even university men as he was. Notably, Washington and Franklin and Henry did not go to college. But how quietly and inevitably Washington came into his stature, and maintained it, compared to the noisy pages of Adams's epic.

John Adams was the son of a New England farmer. He was graduated from Harvard at twenty, and while waiting to choose a profession, accepted a position as teacher in a grammar school in Worcester. But though he held the book, and

no doubt the birch, over the youngsters, there was
nothing mean and lowly in the nature of his
thoughts or the scope of his aspirations. Bursting
on the scene, as he did, to the accompaniment of
the crash of an earthquake, he reveals a mind continually busy with speculation on the large affairs
of life, which he sometimes applied to his own
drama:

"I sometimes in my sprightly moments consider
myself, in my great chair at school, as some dictator
at the head of a commonwealth. In this state I can
discover all the great geniuses, all the surprising
actions and revolutions of the great world, in minia-
ture. I have several renowned generals but three
feet high, and several deep projecting politicians in
petticoats. I have others catching and dissecting
flies, accumulating remarkable pebbles, cockle
shells, &c., with as ardent curiosity as any virtuoso
in the Royal Society. Some rattle and thunder
out A, B, C, with as much fire and impetuosity as
Alexander fought, and very often sit down and cry
as heartily upon being outspelt, as Cæsar did, when
at Alexander's sepulchre he recollected that the
Macedonian had conquered the world before his
age. At the table sits Mr. Insipid, foppling and
fluttering, spinning his whirligig, or playing with

his fingers, as gaily and as wittily as any French coxcomb brandishes his cane or rattles his snuff-box. At another sits the polemical divine, plodding and wrangling in his mind about 'Adam's fall, in which we sinned all,' as his primer has it. In short my little school, like the great world, is made up of kings, politicians, divines, L. D.'s, fops, buffoons, fiddlers, sycophants, fools, coxcombs, chimney sweepers, and every other character drawn in the history of the world."

Thus early, his life-long fashion of leaving others a little breathless, but never himself. Thus early his blustering verbosity, as later he said of his beloved Otis, "left no elbow room" in the conversation. Thus, too, the serious and philosophical youth appeared father of the serious and philosophical man, but not without an occasional twinkle in his eye; and already a non-conformist in daring to coin the obvious and yet undefined word "foppling." Adams thus often made his own verbal tools when none other was at hand; as when he confessed to four successive days devoted to "gallanting the girls," and, on another occasion, when finding himself on horseback and from home, he "oated at Doty's."

He seems to have begun his diary as if it were

a confessional in which he might shrive his soul. "I am constantly forming but never executing good resolutions." . . . "Oh, that I could wear out of my mind every mean and base affectation; conquer my natural pride and self-conceit; expect no more deference from my fellows than I deserve; acquire that meekness and humility which are the sure mark and characters of a great and generous soul; subdue every unworthy passion; and treat all men as I wish to be treated by all." . . . "Vanity, I am sensible, is my cardinal vice and cardinal folly; and I am in continual danger, when in company, of being led an *ignis fatuus* chase by it, without the strictest caution and watchfulness over myself." . . "Dreamed away the afternoon." . . . "Kept school. I am now entering on another year, and I am resolved not to neglect my time as I did last year. I am resolved to rise with the sun, and study the Scriptures on Thursday, Friday, Saturday and Sunday mornings, and to study some Latin author the other three mornings. Noons and nights I intend to read English authors. This is my fixed determination; and I will set down every neglect and every compliance with this resolution. May I blush when I suffer one hour to pass unimproved. I will rouse my mind and fix my attention; I will stand collected within myself, and think upon what I read and what I see; I will strive, with all my soul, to be something more than persons who have had less advantages than myself." A bit of the publican? But honest, for the next day he sets down his failure; "Rose not till seven o'clock. This is the usual fate of my resolutions." Then follow on different days: "I know not what becomes of these days." . . . "I seem to have lost sight of the object that I resolved to pursue. Dreams and slumbers, sloth and negligence, will be the ruin of my schemes."

Not less was his diary the mirror in which he dressed his mind. In it he repeats his recollections of what he has studied or read or heard; his deductions and variations; but there is a continual recurrence of the confessional mood:

"I can as easily still the fierce tempest or stop the rapid thunderbolt, as command the motions and operations of my own mind. I am dull and inactive, and all my resolutions, all the spirits I can muster are insufficient to rouse me from this senseless torpitude. My brain seems constantly in as great confusion, and wild disorder as Milton's chaos; they are numb, dead. I have never any bright refulgent ideas. Everything in my mind appears dim and obscure, like objects seen through a dirty glass or roiled water." There are of course plenty of medicines for such disorders. But he seems not to have taken any, for next day again he was deep in the doldroms of disappointment:

"All my time seems to roll away unnoticed. I long to study sometimes, but have no opportunity. I long to be master of Greek and Latin. I long to prosecute the mathematical and philosophical sciences. I long to know a little of ethical and moral philosophy. But I have no books, no time, no friends. I must therefore be contented to live and die an ignorant obscure fellow."

Though one is inclined more to be amused than sympathetic with self-pity, these are the honest vigorous complaints of one who dares to plant his feet on rugged places. No complacency there, at least. The fact is of course pretty obvious that young Adams had a bad case of New England conscience. Searching and honest, it rode and whipped and spurred him unrelentingly. But it developed his vigorous, powerful mentality; stimulated his ambitions; though it failed to stay some little vanities, and it could not overcome some occasional jealousies. Those rocked but they never wrecked his reputation, because his character and his career were based on honor and energy, fearlessness and fidelity, from which rose a kind of frantic determination when the business of freeing the colonies was concerned.

Adams's mind was avid for information, a maw into which from youth to old age he poured an unceasing stream of reading. During his teaching days he summed his week's reading on Sunday: "Since last Sunday I have wrote a few pages of the Spectator; read the last part of Butler's Analogy; wrote out the tract on Personal Identity, and that upon the Nature of Virtue," and to it adds: "A poor week's work!" Again: "This week I have read one volume of Duncan Forbes's works, and one half of Bentley's Sermons at the Boilean Lectures." At that time he was not yet decided to abandon the pulpit for the bar. At the end of another seven days: "This week I have wrote the eighth Sermon of Bentley's Boilean Lectures. Read part of the first volume of Voltaire's Age of Louis XIV. I make poor week's work." Ever driving himself and complaining of himself.

After his admission to the bar he drew up, in October, 1759, a sort of agenda of study: "It is impossible to judge with much precision, of the true motives and qualities of human actions or of the propriety of rules contrived to govern them, without considering with like attention all the passions, appetites, affections, in nature from which they flow. An intimate knowledge, therefore, of the intellectual and moral world is the sole foundation on which a stable structure of knowledge can be erected. And the structure of British laws is composed of such a vast and various collection of materials, taken partly from Saxony, Normandy, and Denmark, partly from Greece and Rome, and partly from the Canon and Feudal law, that 'tis impossible for any builder to comprehend the whole vast design, and see what is well, and what is ill contrived and jointed, without acquainting himself with Saxon, Danish, Norman, as well as Greek and Roman history, with Civil, Feudal and Canon law.

"Besides all this, 'tis impossible to avail ourselves of the genuine powers of eloquence, without examining in their elements and first principles, the force and harmony of numbers as employed by the poets and orators in ancient and modern times, and without considering the natural powers of imagination and the disposition of mankind to metaphor and figure, which will require the knowledge of the true principles of grammar and rhetoric and of the best classical authors."

A large order, but he rolled up his metaphorical sleeves and tackled it. A few instances stenographically suggest his efforts:

"Begun in pursuance of the foregoing plan, to transcribe from Brighthead's Grammar. I have begun, too, to compare Dr. Cowell's Institutes of the Laws of England, with Justinian's Institutes of the Laws of Rome, title by title. . . .

"By a constant dissipation among amusements in my childhood, and by the ignorance of my instructors in the more advanced years of my youth, my mind has laid uncultivated; so that at twenty five, I am obliged to study Horace and Homer! . . .

"Let me remember to keep my chamber, not run abroad, my books,—Naval Trade, Coke, Andrews, Locke, Homer,—not fields, and groves, and springs, and rocks, should be the object of my attention.

"I began Pope's Homer, last Saturday night was a week, and last night, which was Monday night, I finished it. Thus I find that in seven days I could have easily read the six volumes, notes, preface and essay—that on Homer, and that on Homer's battles, and that on the funeral games of Homer and Virgil, &c. Therefore, I will be bound that in six months I would conquer him in Greek, and make myself able to translate every line in him elegantly."

Yet at the end of the twelve months he confesses and complains and scourges again: "Another year is now gone, and upon recollection I find I have executed none of my plans of study. I cannot satisfy myself that I am much more knowing, either from books or men, from this chamber or the world, than I was at least a year ago. . . . Most of my time has been spent in rambling and in dissipation. Riding and walking, smoking pipes and spending evenings, consume a vast proportion of my time. . . . But I must stay more at home, and commit more to writing. A pen is certainly an excellent instrument to fix a man's attention and to inflame his ambition."

At the other end of his life, when his greatest ambitions had all been realized, and he sat by his chimney-side waiting the call, he still kept up that unremitting quest for knowledge. He had confessed to having "spent an estate in books." In that fascinating correspondence with Jefferson, when Adams was easing down from his seventy-eighth to his ninety-first and last year, he disclosed himself still the omnivorous devourer of books.

Once he took his nose out of the twelve volumes of Dupuis' *Origine de tous les Cultes* to write reams about it to "the young fellow" of Monticello; and at another he slams shut the last volume of Grimm to exult: "I have read Grimm in fifteen volumes, of more than five hundred pages each. I will not say, like Uncle Toby, 'you shall not die' till you have read him, but you ought to read him, if possible. It is the most entertaining work I have ever read." One year Jefferson kept tab on all that Adams had read, and marveled: "Forty-three volumes read in one year, and twelve of them quarto! Dear sir, how I envy you. Half a dozen octavos in that space of time, are as much as I am allowed."

Such an appetite and such energy, evident so early in youth, fed, and quite naturally was fed by, his ambition. Though he spent his young manhood transcribing sermons and listening "all day Sunday" to them, he later shook off "churchliness." But a deep residuum of stabilized character had been formed, a stern honesty of purpose and a vigorous mentality, even if he was unable wholly to discipline his ambition or curb his little vanities. Ambition was a word that he used unsparingly.

When he entered upon the practise of law in

1758, in his twenty-third year, it was a mere vestibule to public political life. At twenty-nine he married Abigail Smith who proved herself one of the great women of her period, of a family to increase Adams's social position, of a character and mentality to provide the understanding and sympathy and aid which he needed.

There has been a disposition in some places to suggest that Adams owed his success in life in a large measure to Abigail. It is scarcely overstatement to say that it has been hinted that Abigail Adams was responsible for all the mistakes John Adams didn't make. Without disparagement of this able and excellent woman, such inferences are not well founded.

His public career divides itself into three parts: before, during, and after his foreign service. The ocean separated him from his wife during the first seven of the ten years he spent abroad. During those seven years were consummated the ablest and most valuable achievements of his work abroad— the straightening out of our French mission, the Dutch treaty and loan, French recognition of American independence, and the English treaty terminating the war and acknowledging the independence of the new nation. Nothing of all his superb achievement in the Continental Congress surpassed these, and certainly nothing he did as President approached them, unless one except his success in warding off the war with France. What Abigail may have prevented his doing as President is another and a speculative matter.

Separated from his wife for long periods, he wrote her letters of all he did, of the personages he met and their character, often with scathing candor, and she wrote him with a firmness and sense that disclosed an intellect only a little less vigorous than his own. He did not follow others, including Washington and Jefferson, in destroying their letters to their wives. But neither Martha Washington nor Jane Jefferson was any part of the intellectual mate for her husband that Abigail Adams was for John.

He was leading, for the most part, in every patriotic movement that developed in New England during his lifetime. By the time he was elected to sit for Massachusetts in the First Continental Congress, he sensed something of the position he was to occupy in public life. His diary took on a new manner as if he believed himself destined for a greatness that would require a biographer, and he would do nothing to withhold the data. He wrote his wife to preserve his letters: "They may exhibit to our posterity a kind of picture of the manners, opinions, and principles of these times of perplexity, danger and distress." Into the ear of his other confidant, his diary, he whispered: "Let me ask my own heart, have I patience and industry enough to write a history of the contest between Britain and America?"

In a large part of all he wrote in letters and diary Adams was voluminously subjective, in marked distinction, for instance, to the reticent objectivity of Washington, who, in his diary, noted, in briefest skeleton form, the weather, the crops and the guests he entertained and the visits he made, with never the lifting for one moment of the curtain of his mind and heart. Adams wrote of every one, with a candor that sometimes swung into complaint, with grumbling and growling, laying about him with a cudgel, to some good or to no good, naively self-revealing most of the time. His writings, as did his utterances, left many bumped pates and barked shins, but no one was left seriously injured, unless it were the old boy of Braintree himself. But, if no one was hurt, he made enemies and made himself vulnerable to their criticism of him. When one has read all that he poured into his criticism of others, however, one somehow feels that one thereby has learned more about Adams than about his victims.

When in Paris, with Franklin and Deane, he was mightily tickled when the tactful honeying French told him that he was "the Washington of negotiation," and he wrote in his diary, "A few of these compliments would kill Franklin, if they should come to his ears." One can scarcely imagine a first-class contemporary of Adams committing himself and his pen to that; but how human of Adams even if not quite believable of Franklin.

Though Adams early admitted vanity among his frailties and strove to discipline it, his political enemies vigorously "admit" that he failed. To that indictment they add the charge of a hearty jealousy of those who raised themselves to a prominence that he coveted. They would have said of Adams, as Adams said of a certain strutting Justice: "His soul is as much swollen as his carcass." In seeking for barbs to annoy him, however, they overlooked the opening given by the minister who married him to Abigail, and for a text chose Luke vii:33, which is given here in the terms said then to have been used: "For John came neither eating bread nor drinking wine, and ye say, *He hath a devil.*"

PATRIOTS OFF THEIR PEDESTALS

This devil in John received its most explicit definition, perhaps, in Hamilton's celebrated indictment of him:

"He is a man of an imagination sublimated and eccentric; propitious neither to the regular display of sound judgment, nor to steady perseverence in a systematic plan of conduct; and I began to perceive what has since been too manifest, that to this defect are added the unfortunate foibles of a vanity without bounds, and a jealousy capable of discolouring every object." One pinch of the salt of fact makes that morsel less unpalatable. It was in fact campaign stuff.

Peppery-tempered Ralph Izard, of South Carolina, rolled all his complaints of Adams into one volley and fired it at him as "His Rotundity." Maclay, a Pennsylvania Senator of the opposite party, who, like Izard, sat and squirmed under Adams's presidency of the Upper House, writhed and wriggled through a diary of his experience there, and, for his most withering sneer, invented the nickname "Bonny Johnny." It is hard wholly to hate a man who inspired from his enemies such nicknames as "His Rotundity" and "Bonny Johnny." The portrait is Pickwickian. The laugh may be on him, but scarcely against him.

JOHN ADAMS

English Thomas Twining, keen and dispassionate, came and observed Adams, and found him, on the other hand, "superior to all sense of superiority." Richard Henry Lee assayed him "sensible and honest" and "rather modest than assuming." Between such divergence it may be believed that the truth lies rather farther than nearer the Hamilton estimate.

Adams's chief jealousy was of Washington. He was militant, but not military. He valued Washington as a soldier, but he did not in advance recognize in the military commander the talents of the civil executive. When the choice of a first President became imminent, Adams, lately at home from his own greatest achievements in Holland, France and England, seems to have dramatized himself as the inevitable civil head of the new state. Yet his disappointment in seeing Washington the choice of the entire nation for the supreme seat, and himself for the merely "respectable situation" of Vice-President, however long it may have lingered, did not cause him to withhold his admiration or his support from his chief.

If Adams was not military by nature and understanding, he was not lacking in bravery. He cast off chips of valor at whatever undertaking his ax whacked. Less significant than his braver performances before and after on larger scenes, but more amusing, is the story, repeated by Charles Francis Adams, of one of his grandfather's sea voyages in connection with his European missions, made on a ship commanded by Commodore Samuel Tucker:

"Discovering an enemy ship, neither Commodore Tucker nor Mr. Adams could resist the temptation to engage, although against the dictates of prudent duty. Tucker, however, stipulated that Mr. Adams should remain in the lower part of the ship, as a place of safety. But no sooner had the battle commenced, than he was seen on deck, with a musket in his hands, fighting as a common marine. The Commodore peremptorily ordered him below; but, called instantly away, it was not until a considerable time had elapsed that he discovered this public minister still at his post, intently engaged in firing upon the enemy. Advancing, he exclaimed, 'Why are you here, sir? I am commanded by the Continental Congress to carry you safely to Europe, and I will do it,' and seizing him in his arms, forcibly carried him from the scene of danger."

Adams left his own account of a less militant

mood in his amiable submission to Benjamin Franklin's persuasions, during a journey they were making together in 1776:

"At Brunswick, but one bed could be procured for Dr. Franklin and me, in a chamber little larger than the bed, without a chimney, and with only one small window. The window was open, and I, who was an invalid and afraid of the night air, shut it close.

" 'Oh,' says Franklin, 'don't shut the window, we shall be suffocated.'

"I answered I was afraid of the evening air. Dr. Franklin replied,

" 'The air within this chamber will soon be, and indeed is now, worse than that without doors. Come, open the window, and come to bed, and I will convince you. I believe you are not acquainted with my theory of colds?'

"Opening the window, and leaping into bed, I said I had read his letters to Dr. Cooper, in which he had advanced, that nobody ever got cold by going into a cold church or any other cold air, but the theory was so little consistent with my experience, that I thought it a paradox. However, I had so much curiosity to hear his reasons that I would run the risk of a cold. The Doctor then began a harangue upon air and cold, and respiration and perspiration, with which I was so much amused that I soon fell asleep, and left him and his philosophy together, but I believe they were equally sound and insensible within a few minutes after me, for the last words I heard were pronounced as if he were more than half asleep."

There came a time when the years, by their own inevitable processes, eliminated all Adams's enemies as well as the objects of all his little jealousies and suspicions, and left him and one other alone among the elder patriots who had resented the English taxes laid without American consent, and had stirred the people to a sense of their wrongs, and had hewed out a new nation. The other was Jefferson.

There had been bad blood there, too. Not at first, in the Continental Congresses where independence was originally considered and then declared, but afterward, when Washington had had two terms in the Presidency and Adams, Federally inclined, found himself saddled with Republican Jefferson as his Vice President; and afterward when Jefferson beat him out of the coveted second term and Adams resentfully spent his last night in office signing the appointments of the "midnight judges," and at dawn fled ill-naturedly from the White House, northward, unwilling to witness the inauguration of his rival.

The two were now old, without further ambitions, or rivalry, or other non-essentials, and with only the realities before them. Then another John Adams came forward, perhaps always the real one, such as Abigail and the children and his other intimates knew, but who had been obscured by the passions and clamor of the public arena. Still restless and curious, still peppery and prodigious in his quest of knowledge, but unafraid to open his heart and declare his affections, it is singular the litany of love he poured out upon his ancient enemy.*

Over and over again he subscribed himself "Your affectionate friend," varying with

"I am in perfect charity, your old friend . . ."

"I am with ancient and friendly sentiments . . ."

"When writing to you I never know when to stop . . ."

"Sick or well the friendship is the same of your old friend . . ."

---

*Correspondence of John Adams and Thomas Jefferson, selected with comment by Paul Wilstach.

"Your assured friend . . ."

"I pray you accept the unabated friendship of your humble servant . . ."

"Wishing your health may last as long as your life, and your life as long as you desire it, I am etc. . . ."

"Your ever affectionate friend . . ."

"So believes your old friend . . ."

"You see, as my reason and intellect fail, my imagination grows more wild and ungovernable, but my friendship remains the same," and his last salute was:

"My love to all your family and my best wishes for your health."

So the sun of this great patriot and able man, with his overwhelming excellencies, his vanities dimmed, his jealousies forgotten, his enemies forgiven, sank in a rosy glow of amiability; energetic amiability of course, in spite of his ninety-one years, for John Adams did nothing that he did not do with forthright honest vigor.

VI

THOMAS JEFFERSON

Is IT possible for the same person to admire both Alexander Hamilton and Thomas Jefferson? If one reads Jefferson on Hamilton, or Hamilton on Jefferson, possibly not. If one reads Jefferson's biographers and Hamilton's biographers, probably not. If one wades and wallows in the bogs of politics contemporaneous with them and trolls the muddy streams of controversy which for more than a century and a third have trailed away from these sources, surely not. Between the steady fire of two sides, between barrages of charge and counter-charge, one is bound to be bewildered. It is the most enduring feud of American political history.

It is only behind the lines, by adhering to one camp or another, that one can find peace of mind about these two great patriots. Either that, or, by declaring a plague on both their houses, leaving both of them on their respective pedestals, and going to hunt the men behind their effigies, does one find realities beyond cavil and personalities which please.

Jefferson was a dreamer. Beauty, ingenuity, theories, projects, all fascinated him, and disclosed him at his best. When they plunged him into conflict with others they showed him at much less than his best. His consciousness of this kept him out of public debate. It seems to have kept him out of any form of discussion even, if one accepts this testimony of Judge Francis T. Brooke, who was a contemporary and an intimate:

"Mr. Jefferson never would discuss any proposition if you differed with him, for he said he thought discussion rather rivetted opinions than changed them."

Philosopher, scientist, artist and writer were rôles he played to his own greatest satisfaction. "I was always fond of philosophy even in its drier forms," he wrote while still a youth. At other times his letters declare: "Nature intended me for the tranquil pursuits of science, by rendering them my supreme delight"; science "is my passion," politics "is my duty"; and he said nothing lured him from such studies but his "revolutionary duties." His farm manager remembered him as "nearly always busy on some plan or model." He was, indeed, a kind of Virginian Benjamin Franklin.

In composing his own epitaph he showed that he believed his fame was securest as author of the Declaration of Independence and of the Virginia Statute for Religious Freedom, and as the Father of the University of Virginia. Leaving the last two achievements to the state for whom they were fashioned, an admiring nation envisages him with the Declaration of Independence as his pedestal.

Off that pedestal he wrote a book, modestly entitled *Notes on Virginia,* descriptive of Virginia when that name applied to a geographical triangle whose apex touched the Atlantic Ocean at the mouth of Chesapeake Bay and whose opposite angles spread until their base disappeared beyond range after range of mountains in hazy wildernesses which no one defined. Like Washington and Adams he was a zealous diarist. Unlike Adams the personal note was entirely omitted; like Washington he was impersonal in his record, but he devoted it almost exclusively to scientific data: to temperature and climate, to plants and animals, to facts and figures about everything that entered practically into his domestic life. He kept tables and schedules with meticulous care. One example

gave the earliest and latest appearances of thirty-
seven varieties of green vegetables in the Washington market during the entire eight years of his two
administrations as President. His agricultural
observations appeared under seventeen general
heads which embraced more than fifty subdivisions;
although he could not make his farms pay.

His private correspondence was prodigious, and
no topic seemed a stranger to it. He even wrote
poetry, but wisely little. The American Philosophical Society elected him its President. He
practised law as an expediency for living. In his
day the bar was the stepping-stone of any young
man of parts into politics. He was drawn in from
no other motive than a career. That career was
stormy and is still a subject of controversy.

His scientific pursuits creep into every period
of his life. While in Congress he invented a copying press, a traveling writing desk, and a multi-
graph writing machine, and prepared and proposed
the unit and coinage of United States money.
While Minister to France he studied grape and
olive culture with a view to introducing those fruits
across the Atlantic; he smuggled an improved rice
out of Italy for the rice planters of the Southern
States; and he discovered the mathematical rule on

the basis of which he invented the mold board of a plow. During other years, in Washington or at home at Monticello, he interested himself in simplified spelling; in the measurement of adjacent mountain altitudes from the top of his own mountain; and in experiments to decide the relative economy between the use of candles and oil lamps. He was, moreover, the first to introduce Merino sheep and threshing machines into America; he devoted thirty years of his life to the making of fifty Indian vocabularies; and he installed in Monticello, of his own contrivance, alcoves for bedding without bedsteads; a bed for himself which disappeared in the ceiling; a "whirligig chair"; adjustable bookcases; a weathervane on the roof which recorded the shifting of the winds on a dial in the ceiling of his portico so that he might know the weather without going into it; and a dual-faced clock in the wall of his house so that from it he could tell the time outdoors as well as indoors.

The loftiest as well as the most extensive employment of his artistic and scientific talents was in architecture. Jefferson was the first great American architect, although he never employed his art except as an amateur. While he was a youth, a copy of the plates of the Italian classicist, Palladio, came into his hands and became his inspiration. From them he absorbed one plate and adapted it to his own use in building his beautiful mansion, Monticello; and from another of Palladio's plates he drew the plans for a house to rise on the site of his birthplace, Shadwell, a plan, however, which was never carried into effect. Palladio's plate from which he took Monticello became also the source of his elaborate scheme, which he supervised in building, for the University of Virginia. He either drew the plans, or supervised the style, for a long list of houses in the neighborhood of Monticello. Among these the best authenticated are Bremo, Barbourville and Farmington. The lofty pillared portico which came into American domestic architecture at the close of the eighteenth century is generally credited either to Jefferson's design or to his influence.

While he was Minister to France he took a long journey to the south of that country. He turned back only after reaching Milan in what may have been an effort to reach Vicenza, the Mecca of all true Palladians. But he visited Nîmes, and there spent many days "gazing whole hours at the Maison Carrée, like a lover at his mistress . . . not without a precedent in my history. While in

150

Paris I was violently smitten with the Hotel de Salm." He intended the dome of the Hotel de Salm for Monticello, but later fell in love with the Temple of Vesta, out of Palladio, and adapted that to his own home.

The hours spent gazing at the Maison Carrée at Nîmes were not without their later influence on American architecture, for when the new state of Virginia asked Jefferson to suggest a plan for its state-house, he redrew the Maison Carrée to scale, adapted it to the requirements of a house of legislature, and his plans were adopted and reproduced in the classic building which has ever since housed the state officials of the Old Dominion.

As Secretary of State in Washington's Cabinet he wrote the program for the competition for plans for the federal buildings in the projected city of Washington. He even submitted his own drawings for a Capitol building. Though that one was not accepted, Jefferson was influential in the choice of Doctor William Thornton's plan, and so, also, in the determination of the classic type which distinguishes our oldest and many of the new national buildings.

Severe and earnest as Jefferson was in the larger projects of his career, in his more intimate moments there was an unmistakable cheeriness of disposition. Among men he seems rather to have "transgressed on the extreme of stiff gentility or lofty gravity" as Maclay put it down in his diary. His gaiety he reserved oftener for women and children.

It is true there are exceptions to his gravity even in contact with men. He must have raised a roar with his imperishable remark about office-holders: "Few die and none resign."

France especially seems to have leavened his nature. Much that he and Benjamin Franklin did will be forgotten when it will still be remembered that when, on Jefferson's arrival in Paris, the Count de Vergennes asked, "You replace Monsieur Franklin?", he replied, "I succeed him. No one can replace him."

When he was homesick he wrote to a lady who lived in the neighborhood of Monticello, begging that she would tell "who dies, that I may meet these disagreeable events in detail, and not all at once when I return; who marry, who hang themselves because they cannot marry."

Of the public wanting more of what they already had too much, he let drop: "They are like a dropsical man calling for water." He gave a three-line portrait of a neighbor's wife in a letter telling of her death: "This last event has given him [the survivor] three quarters of the earth elbow-room, which he ceded to her, on condition she would leave him quiet in the fourth."

Perhaps it ought not to be forgotten that the tradition in Monticello neighborhood is that when on his death-bed, and he awoke and found the physicians consulting over him, Jefferson allowed himself this morsel of grim humor: "Whenever I see three doctors I generally look out for a turkey buzzard."

He wrote himself down frequently as valuing good-humor. To his grandson, Eppes, he said: "Above all things practice yourself in good-humor." "I value more than all other things, good-humor," he said in a letter to his friend, Doctor Rush. "For thus I estimate the qualities of the mind: 1, good-humor; 2, integrity; 3, industry; 4, science." He embroidered a bit on the importance he attached to this virtue, in terms which are somewhat explained by the fact that they were contained in a letter addressed to another grandson:

"I have mentioned good-humor as one of the preservatives of our peace and tranquility. It is among the most effectual, and its effect is so well imitated, and aided, artificially, by politeness, that this also becomes an acquisition of first-rate value. In truth, politeness is artificial good-humor; it covers the natural want of it, and ends by rendering habitual a substitute nearly equivalent to the real virtue. It is the practice of sacrificing to those whom we meet in society all the little conveniences and preferences which will gratify them, and deprive us of nothing worth a moment's consideration; it is the giving a pleasing and flattering turn to our expressions, which will conciliate others, and make them pleased with us as well as themselves. How cheap a price for the good will of another! When this is in return for a rude thing said by another, it brings him to his senses, it mortifies and corrects him in a most salutary way, and places him at the feet of your good-nature in the eyes of the company."

Jefferson's heart seems to have been peculiarly open to children, at least to his own. He is represented by his letters as much more the paternal figure than any of the others of his great coterie. Perhaps this is accented by the fact that many of Jefferson's letters to his children survive as a testimony of such a tenderness, whereas the father-and-children correspondence of the others is meager, when it exists at all. Washington and Madison were childless. Franklin left few souvenirs of his daughter, and he certainly found little consolation in his son, who not only did not follow his father in the great enterprise of the independence of the colonies but gave him the supreme disappointment and humiliation of seeing him espouse the royal cause against the revolution. John Adams seems to have survived apart from his children, stoically keeping private his affection for them, though he was unable to constrain his pride in his son, President John Quincy Adams. The souvenirs of Hamilton as a father are negligible. Of Henry's relations with his numerous family of children there is not more. Though Marshall's ten married years yielded him ten children, they are far in the background of their father's letters and traditions as handed on by him and those who knew him. It is, of course, fair to believe that the children of Hamilton, Henry and Marshall warmed and colored their fathers' lives. The evidence of it is, however, obscure. Jefferson alone left letters which attest a strong paternal instinct, a nature beckoning and bending continually to the two daughters who were the chief delight of his life, as his tenderness to them makes one of the strongest appeals of his private character.

Their names were Martha and Mary; but in their intimacies with their father they were his Patty or Patsy and his Polly. He was not separated from them when he could have them with him. He took Patsy with him when he went as Minister to France, but soon found the separation from Polly was unendurable and with all convenient speed had her too in Paris. When obliged to be separated from them he wrote them continually, generally alternately, and filled his letters with advice and admonitions, the evidences of his love and anxiety for them, his sense of responsibility and his efforts to discharge it, until some one said of him that he acted mother as well as father to his motherless girls.

Patty seems to have erred rather on the side of idleness, for he tried repeatedly to urge her into diligence. One such instance was when he wrote her:

"Of all the cankers of human happiness none corrodes with so silent, yet so baneful an influence, as indolence. Body and mind both unemployed, our being becomes a burthen, and every object about us loathsome, even the dearest. Idleness begets ennui, ennui the hypochondriac, and that a diseased body. . . . If, at any moment, my dear, you catch yourself in idleness, start from it as you would from the precipice of a gulf. You are not, however, to consider yourself as unemployed while taking exercise. This is necessary for your health, and health is the first of all objects. For this reason, if you leave your dancing-master for the summer, you must increase your other exercise."

Again: "Guard at all times against ennui, the most dangerous poison of life. A mind always employed is always happy. The idle are the only wretched. Be good and be industrious and you will be what I shall most love in the world."

Another letter discloses him harping on that "want of industry which I fear will be the rock on which you will split. Determine never to be idle. No person will have occasion to complain of the want of time who never loses any."

Patty may have been an idler, but Polly, in addition to whatever virtues she had, was apparently wilful and obstinate and probably mischievous, all of which, in spite of her father's protests, doubtless endeared the little mad-cap to him all the more. She was kin to the great class of those who just can't write a letter. Her neglect kept her father

begging and threatening. There is such a litany
all through the letters to the children while they
were young:

"I did not write you, my dear Poll, last week,
because I was really angry at receiving no letter.
I have now been nine weeks from home, and have
never had a scrip of a pen. . . . I at first ascribed
it to indolence, but the affection must be weak
which is so long overruled by that." But Poll was
not to be shamed.

"No letter from Maria. I enjoin her as a
penalty that the next shall be in French." There
is no record that she ever paid the penalty.

But when Polly did write, from her aunt's house
near Richmond, whither she had gone visiting, telling of her studies, her reading in *Robertson's
America* and in *Don Quixote,* and of having made
a pudding, her father lost no time in responding
in kind to her newly gracious mood:

"New York, June 13th, 1790.

"My dear Maria—I have received your letter
of May 23d, which was in answer to mine of May
2d, but I wrote you also on the 23d of May, so that
you still owe me an answer to that, which I hope
is now on the road. In matters of correspondence
as well as of money, you must never be in debt. I

am much pleased with the account you give me of your occupations, and the making the pudding is as good an article of them as any. When I come to Virginia I shall insist on eating a pudding of your own making, as well as on trying other specimens of your skill. You must make the most of your time while you are with so good an aunt, who can learn you everything. We had not peas or strawberries here till the 8th day of this month. On the same day I heard the first whip-poor-will whistle. Swallows and martins appeared here on the 21st of April. When did they appear with you? and when had you peas, strawberries, and whip-poor-wills in Virginia? Take notice hereafter whether the whip-poor-wills always come with the strawberries and peas. Send me a copy of the maxims I gave you, also a list of the books I promised you. . . . Adieu, my dear; love your uncle, aunt, and cousins, and me more than all."

He was continually trying to interest both the girls in birds and trees, the seasons and their fruits and flowers, in their language lessons and embroidery and books and music and everything that would make them accomplished women. Sometimes the moral and the amusing became enlaced as in this to Patsy, then in her eleventh year, when obviously she had been frightened of the perennial bugaboo, the end of the world, and wanted to know when the great event was going to happen and what she should do in anticipation of it:

"I hope you will have good sense enough to disregard those foolish predictions that the world is to be at an end soon. The Almighty has never made known to anybody at what time he created it; nor will he tell any body when he will put an end to it, if he ever means to do it. As to preparations for that event, the best way is for you always to be prepared for it. The only way to be so is, never to say or do a bad thing. If ever you are about to say anything amiss, or to do anything wrong, consider beforehand you will feel something within you which will tell you it is wrong, and ought not to be said or done. This is your conscience, and be sure and obey it. Our Maker has given us all this faithful internal monitor, and if you will always obey it you will always be prepared for the end of the world; or for a much more certain event, which is death. This must happen to all; it puts an end to the world as to us; and the way to be prepared for it is never to do a wrong act."

When his daughters were in the country, at Monticello, and he was in the city, either in New

York or Philadelphia, he did their shopping for them, and nothing seems to have been so trifling as to shame him in the doing of it:

"By the stage which carries this letter I send you twelve yards of striped nankeen of the pattern enclosed. There are no stuffs here, of the kind you sent."

"Mrs. Trist has been so kind as to have your calash made, but either by mistake of the maker or myself it is not lined with green. I have, therefore, desired a green lining to be got, which you can put in yourself if you prefer it. Mrs. Trist has observed that there is a kind of veil lately introduced here, and much approved. It fastens over the brim of the hat, and then draws round the neck as close or open as you please. I desire a couple to be made, to go with the calash and other things."

"Instead of waiting to send the two veils for your sister and yourself round [by sailing ship Philadelphia to Richmond] with the other things, I enclose them with this letter. Observe that one of the strings is to be drawn tight round the root of the crown of the hat, and the veil then falling over the brim of the hat, is drawn by the lower string as tight or loose as you please round the neck. When the veil is not chosen to be down, the lower string is also tied round the root of the crown, so as to give the appearance of a puffed bandage for the hat. I send also enclosed the green lining for the calash."

As he addressed himself to each of the virtues—whether it be the employment of time, a course of studies, domestic economy, dress, or the considerations which will aid each of the young ladies as she newly is a wife to come into the happiness which is thus her privilege—he is wise, patient, and finally and frequently tells them that it is all for their happiness which is the only basis of his own. After reading Jefferson's letters to his daughters it needs the assurance of neither of them or of any of their descendants to be confident that among his accomplishments that of parenthood was high.

This gentle paternality was re-accented when Patsy and Polly became Mrs. Randolph and Mrs. Eppes, and supplanted the youthfulness they had grown out of by grandchildren who became the object of his new delight. His frolics with those grandchildren were famous. And when they were separated from him Jefferson wrote of them and then at second hand to them with a sprightly pen. In a letter to Mrs. Randolph, he sent his "best affections" to his son-in-law, and added, apropos their baby: "Anne enjoys them without valuing them."

From the magazines and newspapers he cut anecdotes, jokes, poems and puzzles, and posted them off to the youngsters at Monticello. About to begin a journey home, he wound up a final letter with this allusion to his grandchildren: "The children I am afraid will have forgotten me. However, my memory may perhaps be hung on the Game of the Goose which I am to carry them."

This is the way he gave news to another son-in-law of two other grandchildren: "Francis is now engaged in a literary contest with his cousin, Virginia, both having begun to write together. As soon as he gets to z (being now only at h) he promises to write you a letter." To his daughter who left her children with their grandfather at Monticello, while she rode away to make a round of visits, he gave this news: "Your family of silk-worms is reduced to a single individual. To encourage Virginia and Mary to take care of it, I tell them that, as soon as they can get wedding gowns from this spinner, they shall be married."

As each one mastered the arts of reading and writing he began a correspondence with the grandchildren, as he had with their mothers. A first letter from one of them drew this in reply, which, as a sample, may serve to illustrate all:

"I congratulate you, my dear Cornelia, on having acquired the valuable art of writing. How delightful to be enabled by it to converse with an absent friend as if present! To this we are endebted for all our reading; because it must be written before we can read it. To this we are endebted for the Iliad, the Columbiad, Henriad, Dunciad, and now, for the most glorious poem of all, the Terrapiniad, which I now enclose you." . . . And one can not help wishing the *Terrapiniad* had survived. . . . "I rejoice that you have learned to write, for another reason; for as that is done with a goose-quill, you now know the value of a goose, and of course you will assist Ellen in taking care of the half dozen very fine grey geese which I shall send by Davy." This was Davy Bowles, Jefferson's coachman, who drove the coaches and conveyance wagons back and forth between Monticello and the seat of government.

When away from Monticello and his galaxy of grandchildren his regret frequently crept into his letters and once he reasoned it out thus: "I love to be in the midst of the children and have more pleasure in their little follies than in the wisdom of the wise."

THOMAS JEFFERSON

Though there is no tradition of Jefferson having been a lady's man, there is evidence in his letters that women exhilarated his pen in a way none of his male correspondents did, and that it dashed and scampered for them in a delightfully frolicsome fashion. His Parisian period was his gayest.

The Cosways, English artists, were his particular playmates there. When they returned home across the channel he sent Mrs. Cosway a letter of extraordinary length made up wholly of a sprightly dialogue between his Head and his Heart, in which the former, with an affectation of good sense, upbraids the latter for the romps and time-wastings and moods and foibles into which its affection for her had led him. It is very like, and comparably well done, though infinitely longer than Launcelot Gobbo's dialogue between his conscience and the Devil, which may have suggested it. Another precious example of Jefferson's wit with women, and brief enough for repetition here, is the schedule he wrote another woman of a fashionable Parisienne's day:

"At eleven o'clock, it is day, *chez madame*. The curtains are drawn. Propped up on bolsters and pillows, and her hair scratched into a little order, the bulletins of the sick are read, and the billets of the well. She writes to some of her acquaintance, and receives the visits of others. If the morning is not very thronged, she is able to get out and hobble around the cage of the Palais Royal; but she must hobble quickly, for the *coiffeur's* turn is come; and a tremendous turn it is! Happy, if he does not make her arrive when dinner is half over! The torpitude of digestion a little passed, she flutters half an hour through the streets, by way of paying visits, and then to the spectacles. These finished, another half hour is devoted to dodging out of the doors of her very sincere friends, and away to supper. After supper, cards; and after cards, bed; to rise at noon the next day, and to tread like a mill-horse, the same trodden circle over again. Thus the days of life are consumed, one by one, without an object beyond the present moment; ever flying from the ennui of that, yet carrying it with us; eternally in pursuit of happiness, which keeps eternally before us. If death or bankruptcy happens to trip us out of the circle, it is matter for the buzz of the evening, and is completely forgotten by the next morning."

From Paris, too, he wrote to John Adams's daughter, Mrs. Smith, in answer to her request that he buy her two pair of stays, a formal bit of fooling which wound up with a fine flourish:

THOMAS JEFFERSON

"Mr. Jefferson has the honor to present his compliments to Mrs. Smith and to send her the two pair of corsets she desired. He wishes they may be suitable, as Mrs. Smith omitted to send her measure. Times have altered since Mademoiselle de Sinon had the honor of knowing her; should they be too small, however, she will be so good as to lay them by a while. There are ebbs as well as flows in this world."

When the great Republican wished to bow himself out with a flourish that really flourished, however, his pen was equal to a gesture as wide flung as that of a Molière marquis; as witness this courtesy to the Countess d'Houdetot:

"Repeating to you, Madame, my sincere sense of your goodness to me, and my wishes to prove it on every occasion, adding my sincere prayer that Heaven may bless you with many years of life and health, I pray you to accept the homage of those sentiments of respect and attachment with which I have the honor to be, Madame la Comtesse, your obedient and humble servant."

Nearly all the anecdotes that Jefferson is recorded as having told were about his admired Franklin. One of them which he liked to tell was about how the Doctor was feasted and invited to all the court parties. "At these," said Jefferson, "he sometimes met the old Duchess de Bourbon, who having been a chess player of about his force, they very generally played together. Happening once to put her king in prize, the Doctor took it. 'Ah,' said she, 'we do not take kings so.' 'We do in America,' said the Doctor."

Jefferson probably told another of his stories, one on a certain so-called Count Falkenstein, in connection with that on the Duchess de Bourbon, for it was one which spiced his small talk and flowed naturally from the former anecdote. This so-called Count Falkenstein was in fact the Emperor Joseph II, at the time in Paris incognito under the noble title. He was one of the coterie at the house of the Duchess and is figured as watching the play on the chess-board between her and Doctor Franklin. There was among the rest of the company much talk on "the American question." The Emperor, the Duchess and the Doctor remained in silent concentration on the game.

"How happens it, Monsieur le Comte," asked the Duchess, perhaps before putting her king in prize, "how happens it that while we all feel so much interest in the cause of the Americans, you say nothing for them?"

THOMAS JEFFERSON

"I am a king by trade," replied the candid monarch.

Another of Jefferson's stories of Franklin was told by him in this fashion:

"Dr. Franklin had a party to dine with him one day at Passy, of whom one half were Americans, the other half French, and among the last was the Abbé [Raynal]. During the dinner he got on his favorite theory of the degeneracy of animals, and even of man, in America, and urged it with his usual eloquence. The Doctor at length noticing the accidental stature and position of his guests, at table,

" 'Come,' says he, 'Monsieur l'Abbé, let us try this question by the facts before us. We are here one half Americans, and one half French, and it happens that the Americans have placed themselves on one side of the table, and our French friends are on the other. Let both parties rise, and we will see on which side nature has degenerated.'

"It happened that his American guests were Carmichael, Harmer, Humphreys, and others of the finest stature and form; while those of the other side were remarkably diminutive, and the Abbé himself particularly, was a mere shrimp. He parried the appeal, however, by a complimentary admission of exceptions, among which the Doctor himself was a conspicuous one."

We are in Jefferson's debt for that sidelight on the signing of the Declaration of Independence which shows how the signers are said to have been stung into speeding up their work. His repetitions of this incident made it familiar to many visitors at Monticello during his later years, and one of them, remembering Jefferson's gusto in telling it and the glee of his audience in hearing it, rescued it from the unremembered and unrecorded sidelights on one of the celebrated moments of our history.

Jefferson recalled that near the meeting-place of Congress there was a livery stable. The members wore knee-breeches and silk stockings. It might be noted, though he did not, that those were days before window screens. The southern members at home at their tables were rid of flies by the casual diligence of the slaves who waved paper brushes over their heads; but neither southerner nor northerner in Congress enjoyed any such personal service. The flies from the livery stable swarmed across the street and about the helpless members of the Congress, and attacked their silken shanks. Busy handkerchiefs swished with too little effect. The annoyance dissipated any lethargy attending the ceremony of signing. The sufferers were aroused to an impatience which hurried them into putting down their signatures, and, as they flew before the flies, the consequences on the head of each of them if the great fight failed seem to have been forgotten in the vast and immediate relief to their legs.

The mirror was held up to Jefferson by Maclay more vividly than by any other of his confrères in public life. This Maclay was the first Senator from Pennsylvania, and was the leader of the anti-Federal party before Jefferson came back from France, and, as has been claimed by his Pennsylvania partisans, either deliberately or otherwise Jefferson built the superstructure of his Republican party on the foundations which Maclay had laid. His description of Jefferson was set down in his diary after he came out of a committee meeting where he first encountered the Secretary of State:

"Jefferson is a slender man; has rather the air of stiffness in his manner; his clothes seem too small for him; he sits in a lounging manner, on one hip commonly, and with one of his shoulders elevated much above the other; his face has a sunny aspect; his whole figure has a loose, shackling air. He has a rambling, vacant look, and nothing of that firm, collected deportment which I expected would dignify the presence of a secretary or minister. I looked for gravity, but a laxity of manner seemed shed about him. He spoke almost without ceasing. But his discourse partook of his personal demeanor. It was loose and rambling, and yet he scattered information wherever he went, and some brilliant sentiments sparkled from him. The information which he gave us respecting foreign ministers, etc., was all high-spiced. He had been long enough abroad to catch the tone of European folly." The diarist spiced the reader's appetite, but he withheld the spicy information.

In spite of the long interval of silence, while the bars of resentment were up between John Adams and Jefferson, he did, before and after, write with a sprightly touch to Abigail Adams. He pleaded his inability to find time even for reading as his excuse for not writing oftener, and cited Doctor Franklin, who "used to say that when he was young and had time to read he had no books; and now when he has become old and had books, he had no time." And, at another time, "I have compared notes with Mr. Adams on the score of progeny, and find I am ahead of him and think I am in a fair way to stay so. I have ten and one half grand-children, and two and three quarters great-grand-children, and these fractions will ere long become units."

He was about to be married when he invited a friend to come to Monticello and bring his wife, concluding the letter of invitation with: "Come then and bring dear Tibby with you, the first in your affection, the second in mine." Such was his delight to be relieved of the burdens of state that when Madison succeeded him in the White House, he remained in town and was reported as "never more witty" than at Madison's first reception. When his gay humor was remarked, in contrast with the seriousness of the new incumbent, he explained it with a laugh: "Can you wonder at it? My shoulders have just been freed of a heavy burden, his just laden with it." This was an occasion of which it was banteringly remarked that Jefferson was fêted and followed by the ladies, to which he parried, "That is as it should be, since I am too old to follow them."

In spite of his flippancy with the ladies, Jefferson seems, after the first indecisions of youth when he had given his heart to the Widow Wayles, to have been a man of a single love. He married her in 1772 and she died in 1782. After these ten happy years of companionship with the mother of his two surviving daughters, the succeeding forty-four years, nearly half a century, he devoted to a faithful widowerhood. Yet, in spite of their love and cloudless union, not a single letter to or from his wife was allowed to survive. If any other woman had a sentimental attachment for him, there are no letters to attest it, and nowhere is such a fact remarked by those who knew him.

Jefferson was unquestionably sincere in his belief in decentralization and the people's capacity for self-government, in distinction to Hamilton's belief in a securely centralized government and the obligation of the elect, not to say the élite, to govern the people in their own behalf, and for no other personal quality was Jefferson so well known as for his simplicity. He wore his simplicity as an actor wears a costume, it was his livery of democracy; and at times his emphasis on simplicity became an ostentation. It has been a question whether such ostentation of simplicity shall be thought better than ostentation of ceremonial, and whether both are not mere forms of personal vanity.

His painted portraits disclose no particular evidence of the famous simplicity. The earliest was painted by Mather Brown in 1786 and shows him in his forty-third year. He appears to wear a white wig, and his striped waistcoat opens for a billowing white ruffle. White ruffles also circle the wrists. The general aspect of the man pictured is that of an aristocrat. Trumbell was speaking of the features rather than of the dress, but it is only fair to repeat what he wrote of this picture to Jefferson: "Brown is busy upon the pictures. Mr. Adams is like—yours I do not think so well of." Houdon's bust presents a nicety of dress and coiffure which may be the accent of an artist rather than of his model. It was made in Jefferson's forty-sixth year, while he was Minister to France, and while he was far more intimate with the revolutionists than with the royalists. The subsequent portraits and busts of Jefferson—made in his fifty-seventh year by Gilbert Stuart, in his sixtieth year by Rembrandt Peale and by George Miller, in his sixty-second year by St. Memin, in his seventy-eighth year by Thomas Sully, and in his eighty-second year by Browere—do not disclose sufficient evidence on which to found an opinion of his habits of dress. They do show an increasing carelessness in the adjustment of the dress as well as of the hair, but this may well be the studied indifference of an increasingly great figure or the natural indifference of increasing years. And they may reflect the disposition of the artist to subordinate other details to the countenance.

In his youth assuredly Jefferson was not without a certain fastidiousness. It showed in his foppish concern for the appearance of his riding horses. When a groom brought a horse to his door, Jefferson, before he mounted, would pass a freshly laundered cambric handkerchief over the animal's flank. If the handkerchief showed any evidence of dust the animal was sent back for further polish. A kind of punctiliousness about horses was cultivated by him, or pursued him, throughout life. If, as a democratic pose, which has been but imperfectly authenticated, he rode alone on horseback up to the Capitol to his own inauguration, it is known with certainty that he availed himself at other times of a coach and four. Nor would any horse of any color satisfy his "simple" tastes. His horses were of thoroughbred stock, and none was given a place in his personal service if his coat was other than bay.

There was, moreover, nothing simple about his plan for a home, which envisaged a mansion inspired by and founded on the plans for a palace made by Palladio for Cavaliere Pogliana di

Poligiana, in Vicentini; for which Jefferson supplied nothing less than a mountain for a base. The scale and adornment of Monticello was anything but simple or proletarian. In comparison with it Washington's Mount Vernon and Hamilton's Grange were rather simple and conventional frame houses.

During nearly the whole of the period he spent in Paris, Jefferson lived in the house of Monsieur le Comte de L'Avongeac, on the great boulevard of the Champs Élysées, at the corner of the Rue Neuve de Berry. The mansion, according to one of his family, "was a very elegant one even for Paris, with an extensive garden, court, and outbuildings, in the handsomest style." He must have found life gay and absorbing for, when he had a "press of business," he sometimes fled the Champs Élysées for a Carthusian Monastery on Mount Calvary, whither he took his servant and his papers and remained a week or so in the society of the monks.

While President, and living in the White House, the currents of Jeffersonian simplicity again crossed other currents less simple. His kitchens were under the control of Petit, a French steward he brought from France. The food bill

was reported to have averaged fifty dollars a day
and his wine account summed up to eleven thousand dollars in two terms, which, as prices went in
those days, gives some color to John Adams's
claim that "Jefferson dined a dozen every day" and
"Jefferson's whole eight years was a levee."

He was "very fastidious about the washing and
ironing of his linen"; he wore "silver buckles on
his shoes"; "the servant who attended to his bed-
room was careful to see that well polished shoes
were ready to his hand"; and "whenever a button
came off his apparel he would have it sewed on
with the least delay." This is all reasonable and
conformable to a sound and unaffected simplicity.

There is, however, some contrast between this
simplicity and that of his reception of Mr. Merry,
the British Minister, according to that official's account of his first presentation at the executive
mansion:

"On arriving at the hall of audience we found
it empty, at which Mr. Madison [Secretary of
State] seemed surprised, and proceeded to an entry
leading to the President's study. I followed him,
supposing the introduction was to take place in an
adjoining room. At this moment Mr. Jefferson
entered the entry at the other end, and all three of

us were packed in this narrow space, from which, to make room, I was obliged to back out. In this awkward position my introduction to the President was made by Mr. Madison. Mr. Jefferson's appearance soon explained to me that the general circumstances of my reception had not been accidental, but studied. I, in my official costume, found myself, at the hour of reception he had himself appointed, introduced to a man as the President of the United States, not merely in an undress, but actually standing in slippers down at the heels, and both pantaloons, coat and underclothes indicative of utter slovenliness and indifference to appearances, and in a state of negligence actually studied."

This became one of the historic evidences of Jeffersonian simplicity. The particulars of it were no doubt at once allowed to reach the voting population. It may, however, have been intended as evidence of an unfortunate but deliberate intention to slight the personal representative of a nation which had engaged Jefferson's whole life in a conflict. Perhaps there was in the episode some retaliatory resentment of the indignities which Franklin was made to suffer before the Privy Council and of those reported by John Adams when he was our first Minister to England.

Of Jefferson's simplicity another Englishman remarked recently: "We are not struck by the sincerity of a great nature contemptuous of trifles, but rather by the ingenuity of a great actor who had carefully weighed the value of the meanest accessories." Perhaps; but this commentator is certainly farther from the truth when he calls Jefferson "a kind of Don Quixote; with this difference, that half the world shared his illusions."

When Jefferson saw how well his simplicity, whether it was affected or real, expressed his theories and served his political ends, he seems to have practised it so habitually that it finally became a part of his nature.

A granddaughter witnessed that, in later life, "he paid little attention to fashion, wearing whatever he liked best, and sometimes blending the fashions of several periods. He wore long waistcoats, when the mode was for short; white cambric stocks fastened behind with a buckle, when cravats were universal. He adopted the pantaloon very late in life, because he found it more comfortable and convenient, and cut off his cue for the same reason."

But as a sample of what the repudiation of the conventional may do for a man, nothing else recorded of the so-styled Sage of Monticello quite approaches the display of eccentric simplicity preserved by a visitor to Jefferson's home after the Presidency, who thus described his approach on horseback:

"I was well aware by the cut of his jib who it was. His costume was very singular—his coat was of checkered gingham, manufactured in Virginia I suppose. The buttons on it were of white metal, and nearly the size of a dollar. His pantaloons were of the same fabric. He was mounted on an elegant bay horse going at great speed and he had no hat on, but a lady's parasol, stuck in his coat behind, spread its canopy over his head. . . . This was Thomas Jefferson."

VII

JOHN MARSHALL

In the city of Washington, on the west front of the Capitol building which houses the national legislators and the Supreme Court, there is a statue that seldom arrests the attention of those who are acquainting themselves with that city's revealing treasures, in art or nature, beauty or patriotic significance. The figure is of life size, and the simple pedestal lifts it just above the eye line. There is about it nothing of the heroic. On the contrary there is an easy relaxation in every line of this seated figure loosely wrapped in the judicial gown, even in the cast of thought on the countenance, and in the hand, supported by the arm of the chair, though open in arrested demonstration. This is the statue of John Marshall who was for thirty-four years, from 1801 to 1835, Chief Justice of the Supreme Court of these United States.

There is significance in every feature of this monument's position. It rises on a marble terrace

182

half-way up the tumbling steps which sweep up to the broad white pile, but just below its foundation line. It stands alone; there is not within the Capitol grounds on this side any other human effigy. It centers on the axis of the great familiar dome, an axis which continued westward bisects precisely the nation's supreme tributes to Washington and Lincoln. It may have been accident which so placed John Marshall's statue in the pattern of our Capital City; but it could not have been more appropriately devised.

The bronze figure stands significantly at the base of our temple of supreme law and justice because the decisions he made gave foundation to the Constitution which is the base of our national life. It stands mathematically true to the line which links the heart of the sanctuary of law and legislation to our memorials to Washington and Lincoln, just as he, in the little court room under the great dome, cemented all that Washington and the other fathers fought for, and which the peaceful Lincoln fought another war to preserve.

Washington, Marshall, Lincoln are the three influences in our national history which could have been spared least. And just as this easy modest figure, in the arms of the rises of the great house where is the heart of the nation, must be hunted to be found in its modest but significant position, so Marshall is of all the patriot fathers least obvious to the cursory eye of the reader of history. That destiny would have pleased him, for he was a simple modest man, a domestic figure, except, and perhaps even, when called to the line of public service.

Born in the year 1755 in the Virginia mountain country when it was raw frontier, in his twentieth year he emerged from obscurity to organize a company of minute men and become their leader, and with them he fought in Washington's army in the north. Later choosing the law as his profession, his character was immediately recognized by his own state, which he served as legislator and on the State Executive Council. After his historic success in winning Virginia to the ratification of the Constitution, a success which was shared with Madison, he was offered and refused many national honors; among them the offices of Attorney General of the United States and Minister to France, offered to him by Washington; and by Adams, a seat on the Supreme Bench. Continually pressed, he did serve on a mission to France in 1797-8. The next year he was elected to Congress, but after a few months Adams invited him to become Secretary of War and almost immediately, as the higher office became unexpectedly vacant, to be Secretary of State. This he accepted, and thus he served one year, when the same President named him Chief Justice of the Supreme Court. After that the unity and continuity of his public career were sealed and unbroken.

His statue, the only one raised exclusively to this eminent patriot, by his state or the nation, represents him as the jurist and constructor, contemplative and profound. It represents him as our history and our national security have made him familiar to those few who really know his intellectual force and the massive supports which he placed under the Constitution. Whatever the public, careless of visiting this statue on its low pedestal, may know of him on the supreme bench, they know him almost not at all in his private life.

What must have been the personal character of a man who for thirty-four consecutive years sat, for the most part, listening to arguments of special pleaders, and, for the rest, digging the principle and truth out of the confused mass and setting it up in masterly decisions? How else shall one think of of him except as a pundit, a sage, an oracle; a dry old party cluttered about with dusty briefs and musty tomes, pleas and opinions, red tape and hoary precedents?

Curiously, on the contrary, John Marshall was the cheeriest, blithest spirit of all the early fathers. He looked life, as well as law, eye to eye. He had a well within from which he drew the gay often as the grave. He kept his body supple and strong with fresh air and play. He kept his mind refreshed with laughter and perfumed with the love of his fellow man.

His appearance seems to have been distinguished by his unusual height, by his easy lounging manner and by his brilliant piercing eyes. William Wirt sketched him as "tall, meagre, emaciated, his muscles relaxed, . . . his head and face are small in proportion to his height, his complexion swarthy . . . his countenance expressing great good humor and hilarity; while his black eyes possess an irradiating spirit which proclaims the imperial powers of the mind that sits enthroned within." His fellow-justice Story remarked his "small twinkling eyes," and another contemporary remembered those eyes as "dark to blackness, strong and penetrating, beaming with intelligence and good nature."

Marshall could, however, suppress both twinkle and beam, for it was noted that when a lawyer talked against time or annoyed the court with platitudes, he fastened a cold, wide-open, never blinking eye upon him, and the offender wilted under it. And he knew how to make another use of his eyes, as he explained when he once said that "the acme of judicial distinction" meant to him "the ability to look a lawyer straight in the eyes for two hours and not hear a damned word he says."

All his life he seems to have been careless of his clothes, which appeared not quite to have fitted him, and later as if made not only for some one else but for some one else of a previous generation. His surtout was longish and its capacious pockets were often filled to overflowing with books and documents. But one who knew him in his later days said that a peculiar characteristic of his dress was a long green umbrella, which, rain or shine, was his constant companion. There was nothing of the dandy about Marshall.

He was an outdoors man every year of his long life. In boyhood he shared the hewing and plowing of a frontier farm. It is said that when he was lieutenant of his county's minute men he walked ten miles to the muster field for drills and the same distance back to his father's house. Wishing to be inoculated against smallpox in 1780, at a time when the duration of the war had made horses scarce, and he was about to be married, he walked from Virginia to Philadelphia, averaging, according to his own calculation, thirty-five miles a day.

At the other end of his life, while sitting with the Supreme Court in Washington, he made it his daily practise to rise at daybreak and, before breakfast, walk the length of Pennsylvania Avenue to the Treasury and back to the Capitol, a distance of about three miles. During the Court recesses, which he spent with his family in Richmond, he was accustomed to walk every morning to his farm four miles from town, unless he had some heavy object to carry, when he rode horseback. It was on this farm that, he wrote Monroe, "I pass a considerable portion of my time in laborious relaxation."

He was fond of tying his exercise up to contests. While General Washington's army agonized through the Valley Forge experience, Captain Marshall was accounted one of the best athletes in camp, and led in organizing athletic activities for the General. "He was the only man," said Josiah Quincy, "who with a running jump could clear a stick laid on the heads of two men as tall as himself. On one occasion he ran in his stocking feet with a comrade. His mother, in knitting his stockings, had the legs of blue yarn and the heels of white. This circumstance, combined with his uniform success in the race, led the soldiers . . . to give him the soubriquet of 'Silver Heels.' "

His preferred out-of-door sport all his life was the homely game of pitching quoits. From the time that he was yet a young man in Richmond, but old enough to take the leading rôle in Virginia's Constitutional Convention, he was one of the selected thirty who formed the celebrated Quoit Club, which it was their pride later to say "was as old as the Constitution of the United States." The club met weekly in a grove at Buchanan's Spring, then a mile outside the city. All other members used brass quoits, highly polished. Marshall preferred his own, of rough cast iron, and twice the weight of the others.

There are several engaging pictures of the Chief Justice at the Quoit Club. Chester Harding, the artist, was invited out to see him play, and said: "I watched for the coming of the old chief. He soon approached with his coat on his arm, and his hat in his hand, which he was using as a fan. He walked directly up to a large bowl of mint julep and drank off a tumbler full of the liquid, smacked his lips, and then turned to the company with a cheerful 'How are you, gentlemen?' He was looked upon as the best pitcher of the party and could throw heavier quoits than any other member of the club.

"The game began with great animation. There were several ties and, before long, I saw the great Chief Justice of the Supreme Court of the United States down on his knees, measuring the contested distances with a straw, with as much earnestness as if it had been a point of law, and, if he proved to be in the right, the woods would ring with his triumphant shout."

Sometimes he went at the measuring with knife and teeth as well as straw. Kneeling over the contested quoits he was seen with "the blade of the knife stuck through the straw, holding it between the edge of the quoit and the hub, and, when it was a very doubtful question, pinching or biting off the end of the straw, until it would fit to a hair."

There was a club rule that neither politics nor religion was to be discussed at the barbecue, and the penalty for infraction of the rule was a basket of champagne which would be produced at the next meeting "as a warning to evil doers," and for other purposes. On one such occasion the much cheered members went out into the grove after lunch, and the game was led by Marshall and one Parson Blair. Marshall played first and "rang the meg." The parson followed him and repeated the feat, landing his quoit plump over Marshall's. This was followed by great applause, but developed an animated discussion. The members returned to table as to a court room, fortified themselves with another round of champagne, and listened to the arguments. Marshall appeared in his own behalf, but Wickham, a leading Virginia lawyer, appeared for the parson. The question at issue was: "Who is the winner when the adversary quoits are on the meg at the same time?"

"Marshall's argument is a humorous companion piece to any of his judicial opinions," said one of the perpetuators of the gay incident. "The first one ringing the meg, he argued, had the advantage; no one could succeed who did not begin by displacing him. The parson, he willingly allowed, deserves to rank higher in everyone's esteem, but then he must not do it by getting on his adversary's back. That is more like leap-frog than quoits. . . . His own right as first occupant, extended to the vault of heaven. No opponent can gain any advantage by squatting on his back—he must either bring a writ of ejection or drive him out *vi et armis.* And then, after further argument of the same sort, he asked judgment.

"Mr. Wickham then arose and made an argument of the same pattern. No rule, he said, required an impossibility. Mr. Marshall's quoit is twice as large as any other's, and yet it flies from his arm like an iron ball at the Grecian games, from the arm of Ajax. It is an iron quoit, unpolished, jagged, and of enormous weight. It is impossible for an ordinary quoit to move it. With much more of the same sort he contended that it was a drawn game. After animated voting, protracting the uncertainties as long as possible, it was so decided."

So thoroughly did Marshall enjoy such diversion that, on one occasion, he brought to the club meeting two hams, one boiled in the Maryland fashion and one other boiled in the Virginia fashion, and, after the members had sampled both, he submitted their rival merits to another such mock discussion as amused him so much.

How genuinely he loved the game of quoits is further illustrated by the incident of a picnic in the mountains where a game of quoits was proposed but no quoits were to be had. Marshall was an old man at the time. But, after disappearing from the party for a short time, he reappeared from a thicket bordering on a brook, carrying a pile of flat stones extending from his waist to his chin. He elbowed his way into the crowd, threw down the stones among them, as if issuing a challenge, and the game began.

When Marshall died the gentlemen of the Richmond Quoit Club made no effort to fill his place. The membership afterward remained one less than it had been while he lived.

His own Lawyers' Dinners, in his Richmond home, were famous, among his contemporaries. On those occasions he gathered the leading members of the local bar, usually to the number of thirty. At the head of his table he led in toasts, and stories, and wit, and of course in hearty laughter. He was thoroughly convivial, loving his fellow man and beloved by others. His devotion to games included whist and backgammon, and when alone he read novels and poetry. Occasionally he wrote poems, but, like Jefferson, who also wrote them, he was much too cagey to publish them.

One bit of his rhyming has survived, however,

and Beveridge, having it of one of Marshall's descendants, uses it in illustrating the Chief Justice's sprightly contributions to any informal company of which he was a part. "On one occasion," as Beveridge repeats the story, "he went to the meeting of a club at Philadelphia, held in a room at a tavern across the hall from the bar. It was a rule of the club that every one present should make a rhyme upon a word suddenly given. As he entered, the Chief Justice observed two or three Kentucky colonels taking their accustomed drink. When Marshall appeared in the adjoining room, where the company was gathered, he was asked for an extemporaneous rhyme on the word 'paradox.' Looking across the hall, he quickly answered:

" 'In the Blue Grass region,
    A Paradox was born.
The corn was full of kernels
    And the "colonels" full of corn.' "

Though for over a third of a century he delivered constitutional opinions which have withstood the development and bickerings of over a hundred subsequent years, and in the face of political adversaries who tried in every way to oust him, yet he was incapable of a personal quarrel, even with Jefferson, his bitterest antagonist. In

194

spite of perfect physical and moral courage, others found him, as did Wirt, "a man without an atom of gall in his whole composition." This may have been in part perhaps because, as another has said, "he had not a particle of vanity in his make-up."

The anecdotes of him, which have authentic foundation, illustrate a character of singular fortitude, of generosity, and of meticulous honor, and, in spite of a mind which steered through the fogs of contention directly to the heart of every matter it touched, a disposition which was modest, fun-loving and careless almost to shiftlessness.

Marshall's youth in the backwoods, his years in the field during the war, and his uninterrupted devotion to out-of-door sports, made him equal to any physical endurance. The fortitude he showed on his trip on foot from central Virginia to Philadelphia was equaled by another extraordinary test of his mettle which came toward the end of his life. In his seventy-sixth year, suffering with the stone, he journeyed to Philadelphia and, necessarily without the then unknown anesthetics, he submitted himself to the surgeon's knife. An attending physician who visited him two hours before the operation found him calm and self-possessed, and enjoying a hearty breakfast.

"I thought it very probable that this might be my last chance," said Marshall, "and therefore I was determined to enjoy it and eat heartily."

When he had finished eating he asked how long it would be before the operation, and the doctor said there would be nearly two hours. Whereupon he dismissed the doctor and lay down and slept soundly until he was roused for the operation. In spite of the tedious, dangerous and painful nature of the operation, he endured it without flinching. He had a perfect recovery, and the same trouble never returned.

One of the best illustrations of his frequently noted generosity, was preserved by the collector, Henry Howe. Marshall was once riding through Culpeper County, Virginia, up into Fauquier. On his way he met an old friend whom he had known since the early years in the army. Their conversation developed that the man was anticipating losing his property by the impending foreclosure of a mortgage for three thousand dollars. When Marshall departed he left behind a check for the entire amount, to be given his friend privately after he had gone. His friend, however, when the check was given him, "impelled by a chivalrous independence," mounted his horse and spurred on until he overtook Marshall, when he gratefully but firmly refused to accept such generosity. Each friend persisted in his point of view until a compromise was admitted by which Marshall took security for the sum advanced. The story concludes: "But he never called for the payment," which leaves an inevitable doubt as to whether he ever got it.

His sense of obligation to his judicial position prevented him ever from voting in elections for office while he was on the bench. This same particularity extended to the smallest niceties of private conduct. Bishop Meade, who more than once traveled with him between Fauquier and Fredericksburg, related that "when we were both going to the lower country on one occasion, when we came to that miry part called the 'Black Jack,' we found that the travellers through it had taken a nearer and better road through a plantation. The fence being down, or very low, I was proceeding to pass over, but he said we had better go round, although each step was a plunge, adding that it was his duty, as one in office, to be very particular in regard to such things."

Although modest, he was never shy. He had a bouncing gregarious spirit, yet, when asked for Washington's letter requesting him to enter public life, he reluctantly and only confidentially gave it. When first his *Life of Washington* appeared, in an edition of five ponderous volumes, the English critics were frankly severe. Marshall's American friends rallied to his defense, though that biography was the least admired of his public works. But he himself remained modestly quiet, digested the criticism, and corrected all the errors which had been pointed out, a process which included the hacking away of so much irrelevant material, that he reduced the five volumes to two, in which form it was republished.

Few men probably knew their limitations better than Marshall. He was conscious in particular of his lack of academic learning. As a small boy he was without schooling except such as his father gave him on their frontier farm. But that father gave him principle instead of pedagogy, and ideals which discounted mere ignorance of the insides of books. He was fourteen when he first went to school, and then and after his tuition was intermittent and brief, until he had fought through the first years of the Revolution. His training for the bar included a youthful acquaintance with Blackstone's *Commentaries,* from one of the very first copies to reach America, and six weeks under Chancellor Wythe at Williamsburg.

His mind, however, was a species of self-sufficient mechanism. When he had studied a question he would declare the law, and add to an associate-justice: "Now you find the authorities." In telling of this Story said: "When I examine a question, I go from headland to headland, from case to case; Marshall has a compass, puts out to sea, and goes direct to his result."

This accurate self-appraisement had caused him, shrewdly, when previously practising law, to speak last in defense of any cause. He was willing to avail himself of all points he might pick up from the pleaders who preceded him on either side.

No lawyer who appeared before the bench on which Marshall sat as Chief Justice, and transfixed bores and humbugs with his brilliant unwinking eyes, and wrote opinions fundamental as truth itself and enduring as granite, found in that mentality any reflex of his simple, casual, careless personality at other times. He knew how to be firm and stern, though he seems to have preferred to wrap rebuke in a veil of transparent restraint, as when, a lawyer having started his discourse at the origin of all things and trailed down the ages toward the case in hand, he interrupted the bore with: "Brother, there are some things which a

Chief Justice of the United States may be presumed to know."

Yet there are glimpses of him at a country inn carrying in wood from a woodpile, because, as he explained, "it may not be convenient for [the landlord] to keep a servant, so I make up my own fires"; at another time overcoming the awe of a small boy who came to his office in the Capitol to deliver some papers, by engaging the youngster in a game of marbles on hands and knees; and earlier, while yet a young lawyer, strolling down street in Richmond, "in a plain linen roundabout and shorts," eating cherries out of his hat carried in the crook of his elbow. Out of the last incident developed an anecdote whose repetition caused him considerable satisfaction.

In his usual fashion of easing his way from his house to his office, stopping at front gates and open doors for greetings and gossip, on the morning in question he stopped in the porch of the Eagle House for a word with the landlord and then passed along. Present in the porch was a Mr. P—— from the country, who had come to town to engage an advocate to manage a case for him in the court of appeals. The landlord recommended Marshall, but the suggestion was declined, as the young attorney's easy going ways had made a poor impression. It was said that when Mr. P—— appeared in the court room he was again referred to Marshall, but his prejudice still prevailed. Presently another lawyer, a certain Mr. V—— entered the room. His venerable appearance, his neat black coat and powdered wig, made such an impression that he was engaged at once. In the first case up that day Marshall and Mr. V—— each addressed the Court, and such was the manifest superiority of the younger man that Mr. P—— went to him at the close of the case, admitted his earlier prejudice, regretted his error, but did not know how to get out of his dilemma, for, after engaging and paying the other man, he had but five dollars in his pocket; yet he wanted Marshall to appear for him. The situation amused Marshall so much that he took the case but "not without a sly joke at the importance of a powdered wig and a black coat."

There are other instances of Marshall's appearance deceiving strangers. It is known that, though he may not have affected carelessness in dress for the sake of the fun which he sometimes had of it, he nevertheless enjoyed the situation which it developed.

One morning he went to pay a call on the bride

of his newly married brother. She was expecting the butcher to buy a calf which she had for sale. The servant who answered the door-bell was so little impressed with the caller's appearance that she reported to her mistress that the butcher was at the door. When she brought back word to him that he would find the calf in the stable, he laughingly explained who he was, and was shown into the presence of his much mortified sister-in-law.

Another of these gossipy Richmond traditions tells of how, later in life, he was standing at the entrance of the Market House when a young man, lately come to town, addressed Judge Marshall as "old man" and asked if he would "like to make a nine pence by carrying a turkey home for him?" It was just the sort of prank Marshall enjoyed, and he took the turkey without a word and followed the stranger to his own door.

"Catch!" said the hirer, on their arrival there, tossing nine pence to his hireling.

Marshall caught the coin and pocketed it, and the young man before he had entered his house saw a better-known citizen, in passing, lift his hat with deference to the retreating figure, and asked:

"Who is that shabby old fellow?"

"The Chief Justice of the United States."

"Impossible! Why did he bring my turkey home, and—take—my nine pence?"

"Probably to teach you a lesson in good breeding and independence. He will give the money away before he gets home. You can't get rid of the lesson. And he would carry ten turkeys, and walk ten times as far, for the joke you have given him."

Although he told such stories on himself at his own dinner-table, and led in the laughter, his descendants have demurred somewhat at the occasionally shabby figure thus depicted, and protest that the Chief Justice was little more than old-fashioned in his dress, but always neat, and that he sometimes assumed an "antic disposition" for the fun of the thing. Story found him "neat in his dress," as did other contemporaries who referred to his appearance. Certainly there was no disorder, no shabbiness, no old-fashionedness in the great mind behind the black piercing eyes.

He wrapped up sufficient testimony of how casual he could be, however, in a letter from the circuit to his wife at home in Richmond, and passed it off with his usual gay candor:

"Rawleigh, Jany. 2^d. 1803.
"My Dearest Polly
"You will laugh at my vexation when you hear

the various calamities that have befallen me. In the
first place when I came to review my funds, I had
the mortification to discover that I had lost fifteen
silver dollars out of my waist coat pocket. They
had worn through the various mendings the pocket
had sustained & sought their liberty in the sands
of Carolina. I determined not to vex myself with
what could not be remedied & orderd Peter to take
out my cloaths that I might dress for court when to
my astonishment & grief after fumbling several
minutes in the portmanteau, staring at vacancy, &
sweating most profusely he turned to me with the
doleful tidings that I had no pair of breeches. You
may be sure this piece of intelligence was not very
graciously receivd; however, after a little scolding
I determined to make the best of my situation &
immediately set out to get a pair made. I thought
I should be sans coulotte only one day & that for
the residue of the term I might be well enough
dressed for the appearance on the first day to be
forgotten. But, the greatest of evils, I found, was
followed by still greater! Not a Taylor in town
could be prevailed on to work for me. They were
all so busy that it was impossible to attend to my
wants however pressing they might be, & I have
the extreme mortification to pass the whole time

without that important article of dress I have mentioned. I have no alleviation for this misfortune but I hope that I shall be enabled in four or five days to commence my journey homeward & that I shall have the pleasure of seeing you & our dear children in eight or nine days after this reaches you. In the mean time I flatter myself that you are well & happy.

      "Adieu my dearest Polly

        "I am your ever affectionate

          "J. Marshall."

It is said that he arrived at some of his most profound decisions riding horseback or driving in his one-horse stick-gig over, or perhaps in, the wretched lonely circuit roads, unseen and seeing no human being hour upon hour, undisturbed in the silences of the pine forests. On one such occasion his detached mind was brought back to his situation by the fact that his neglected horse had turned out of the road and run over a sapling, and he discovered himself literally hung up. An old negro found him so, bewildered by his predicament and unable to extricate himself.

"My old master," the tradition quotes the darky as saying, "what for you don't back your horse?"

"That's true," said the judge, and, as he backed out and started off, he felt in his pocket for a bit of change for his deliverer. It is scarcely surprising to be told that he had none.

"Never mind, old man," he said, "I shall stop at the tavern and leave some money for you with the landlord."

The old negro, in spite of his secret opinion of the stranger, did drop in at the tavern, and asked if anything had been left for him by an old gentleman passing that way.

"Oh, yes," said the landlord, "he left a silver dollar for you. What do think of that old gentleman?"

"He was a gemman, for shore, but," tapping his forehead, the negro added, "he didn't have much in there."

This absentmindedness once obtruded on Marshall's public service in a seriously embarrassing manner. It happened while he was Secretary of State. President Adams in the last hours of his administration appointed forty-two justices of the peace for the District of Columbia. It was the Secretary of State's duty to cause their commissions to be delivered to the appointees. With "his customary negligence" for such details Marshall omitted to attend to the matter and returned to his home in Richmond. President Jefferson, deeply chagrined over Adams's filling of the judicial vacancies by these so-called "mid-night judges," declined to recognize the validity of the tenure of some of them, and out of the situation grew one of the most famous cases before the Supreme Court, Marbury vs. Madison, and one of Chief Justice Marshall's most significant decisions.

Justice Story left an ingratiating picture of the communal life of the justices of the Supreme Court under Marshall, and pointed it with another instance of that great man's amiability:

"We take no part in Washington society. We dine once a year with the President, and that is all. On other days we dine together, and discuss at table the questions which are argued before us. We are great ascetics, and even deny ourselves wine except in wet weather.

"What I say about wine gives you our rule; but it does sometimes happen that the Chief Justice will say to me, when the cloth is removed, 'Brother Story, step to the window and see if it does not look like rain.' And if I tell him that the sun is shining brightly, Judge Marshall will sometimes reply: 'All the better, for our jurisdiction extends over so large a territory that the doctrine of chances makes it certain that it must be raining somewhere.' "

Marshall was married in his twenty-eighth year, his wife bore him ten children, and their union endured during forty-eight years until her death. For the greater part of their life together she was an invalid, yet his unfailing love and devotion marked the match as one of the real romances of the early patriots. There is the lavender of a lifetime of love in the letter which he wrote her in his seventieth year. Such a letter in connection with Hamilton's love-letter and the absence of any such survivals from the pen of Washington, Franklin, Henry, Adams, Jefferson or Madison leave us to wonder how romance fired them in their youth and whether when the fulness of their years had overtaken them they found embers worth warming their aging hearts.

Marshall, when he wrote this letter, was in Washington, housed by an injured knee, and, remarking the leisure which the accident gave him, asked his "Dearest Polly" how she thought he beguiled his time, and answered the question for her:

"I am almost tempted to leave you to guess until I write again. You must know that I begin with

the ball at York, and with the dinner on the fish at
your house next day: I then retrace my visit to
York, our splendid Assembly at the Palace in
Williamsburg [all, including what follows, ref-
erences to his courting days], my visit to Richmond where I acted Pa for a fortnight, my return
the ensuing fall and the very welcome reception
you gave me on your arrival from Dover, our little
tifts and makings up, my feelings while Major
Dick was courting you, my trip to the cottage, the
lock of hair, my visit to Richmond the ensuing fall,
and all the thousand indescribable but deeply
affecting instances of your affection or coldness
which constituted for a time the happiness or
misery of my life and will always be recollected
with a degree of interest which can never be lost
while recollection remains."

Marshall died in his eighty-first year in Philadelphia, the city where his services to the law and
Constitution of the land had begun. It was a coin-
cidence, which some regard with sentimental
significance, that it was while tolling the great
jurist's funeral that the Liberty Bell cracked and
has since remained silent.

One of the Presidents said of him: "He found
the Constitution paper and made it a power; he

found it a skeleton and made it flesh and blood."
There is no other man in our history, except perhaps Washington, who has been written of with
such unfailingly high tributes to his great public
service and his attractive private character as
Marshall. Yet from the choir of praise one voice
rises in a tone and in terms that seem to say enough,
if not all.

After twenty-four years' intimate association
with Marshall, sitting with him daily on the
Supreme Bench and living with him in the
Justices' community house, Joseph Story exclaimed: "I am in love with his character, positively
in love," and "He is beloved and revered . . .
beyond all measure, though not beyond his merits.
Next to Washington he stands the idol of all good
men."

VIII

JAMES MADISON

"GREAT LITTLE MADISON." There, in three words, the fascinating Dolly Todd, widowed, and with an eye to correcting that state, gave the character and the portrait of the man who was to become her second husband.

That was in the year 1794, and the forty-fourth of James Madison, Jr. After that, if he was never littler, it is true also that he was never greater. He lived to be eighty-five, but, though he had honors heaped upon him with the ascending years, nothing that he did in the second half of his long life equaled the attainments of his bachelor beginnings.

He was virtually a youngster compared to the majority of the preeminent patriot fathers among whom he won his spurs. Only John Marshall was junior, by four years, and Hamilton, by six. Jefferson was Madison's senior by eight years, Patrick Henry by fifteen, John Adams by sixteen, Washington by nineteen, George Mason by twenty-six,

Samuel Adams by twenty-nine, and Benjamin Franklin by forty-five. Madison was also a youngster in appearance for he was only five feet six inches tall, and weighed but one hundred and twenty-five pounds.

There was little background to "great little Madison." He stands on his pedestal, vivid and vital, a personality of sheer mentality, a mental giant if no physical colossus, perhaps the greatest single figure in the framing and adoption of the Constitution. He spent most of the middle period of his life, before and after the great convention, in Virginia and in national assemblies, and was a leader at all times in the framing of policy and in making his policies prevail. Later he was Jefferson's Secretary of State and that same able political leader's successful candidate for President of the United States.

Off this pedestal Madison is a bit nebulous, if not quite negligible. "As to Jemmy Madison," exclaimed Washington Irving, after attending his Inaugural Ball, "ah! poor Jemmy! he is but a withered little Apple-John." Even the British Minister, "Copenhagen" Jackson, reported Madison "a plain and rather mean-looking little man."

There, on and off, was the best and the worst

of him. Accompanying him, through the high-
ways and byways of his long life, his unpretentious
amiability, however, supported by the very absence
of any trace of intellectual ostentation, withers
Irving's estimate and makes Jackson's look much
meaner than he could possibly have intended.

Beyond the record of Madison's birth at Port
Conway, on tidal Rappahannock, and of some
early tuition under the "learned" Donald Robertson of King and Queen County, there are no
reminiscences of Madison's youth. Perhaps the
cerebral prodigy had no youth. Tradition certainly stints him of it. His parents were well
placed in life, but in the character of neither of
them, so far as known, was there any suggestion
of the extraordinary product of their union. There
is perhaps no accounting for the brilliant progeny
which occasionally springs from safe, sound,
worthy but uninspiring sources. Possibly Madison may be accounted for on the same principle as
"Lighthorse Harry" Lee who, when asked to ex-
plain how two such dull people as his parents produced so distinguished a son, recalled that "two
negatives make a positive."

The earliest written word of Madison's own,
which intervening vicissitudes have left us, is dated

"Nassau Hall, August 16, 1769," and of his years the eighteenth, and reveals him in his first days at Princeton College, one of more than one hundred students, "all in American cloth." In the course of that letter he wrote:

"The near approach of examination occasions a surprising application to study on all sides, and I think it very fortunate that I entered college immediately after my arrival. Though I believe there will not be the least danger of my getting an Irish hint, as they call it, yet it will make my studies somewhat the easier."

He seems not to have received the "Irish hint," for he remained on for two years. Of his college days the few surviving letters are to "Honoured Sir" his father. Young Madison was diffident, frail and obviously a grind, often only allowing himself three hours' sleep. But not quite all his waking hours found him with his nose in books, for there are traditions of his smoking his church-warden pipe and drinking his ale before the blazing logs of the great fireplace of Nassau Inn.

His college contemporaries were a notable company, and, among others, included Brockholst Livingston, later Justice of the Supreme Court of the United States; Henry Lee, later "Lighthorse

Harry"; and one Aaron Burr. In a company
which included these, and other youths who became only a little less celebrated as men, he took a
conspicuous position. He helped to found the
Whig Club, which takes color from "the looped
and flowing ribbon" which the members wore on
their wrists; an early expression, if not actually
the origin, of the wearing of college colors. However, Madison has never been directly accused of
having inaugurated and imposed this fashion of
American student life.

He left Princeton a Bachelor of Arts in 1772,
but not for the last time. He came back, eleven
years later, when the itinerant Congress, driven
north and westward, made Princeton one of the
successive capitals of the rebellious colonies, and
there he led a legislature, in the hall where formerly
he had led the students.

Between Commencement at College and the
beginnings of a career, young Madison spent two
years at his father's house, Montpellier, in Orange
County, in the foot-hills of the Virginia mountains.
He dressed in solemn black, and privately read
theology. "I am dull and infirm," he wrote a
friend, and he did "not expect a long or healthy
life." However, his frail little body carried him

along for eighty-five years, though never into the pulpit.

When he appeared in the Virginia convention of 1776, he was twenty-five, "but," an observer present remarked that, "he did not look twenty-one." At the peak of his career he cut quite another figure. When he and John Marshall met and vanquished George Mason and Patrick Henry in the Virginia Constitutional Convention of 1787, Madison had filled out somewhat. His cheeks were ruddy, his suit was blue and buff, with a straight double collar at the top of his long single-breasted coat, his breeches met his stockings at the knee, his silver shoe buckles were large and conspicuous, and ruffles billowed at his breast and at his wrists. He combed his hair low on his forehead to hide the beginning of baldness, and a ribbon held the rest of his hair gathered behind in "a queue no bigger than a pipe-stem."

In the midst of older men, taller men and louder speakers, this extraordinary little man still managed to dominate. His voice was no bigger than he was. It was remembered that John Randolph rose and advanced several steps, and cupped his hand behind his ear, to hear Madison, but gave it up in despair and returned to his seat. But that small voice eventually commanded his hearers, for Madison achieved a fame for "clear and cunning argumentation." John Marshall, at the evening of his days, recalling that "Eloquence has been defined to be the art of persuasion," added, "And, if it includes persuasion by convincing, Mr. Madison was the most eloquent man I have ever heard."

The fight for the Constitution was the peak of Madison's performance. He was able always, though as President his "army," in the futile defense of the city of Washington in the war with the British in 1814, put him in rather an undignified flight all the way from the firing line in near-by Maryland, across the city and across the Potomac River, to the protection of the Virginia hills. In fact, after his supreme achievements for the Constitution, the rest of his public life was really just recognition and reward. After these rewards, which were eight years in the chair of State and eight years in the White House, he took himself off to Montpellier, there to make himself "a fixture," anticipating in the familiar phraseology of the contemporary Cincinnati returning to their farms, "many enjoyments in exchange for the labors and anxieties of public life."

Nearly every one who knew Madison and wrote

of him testified to his superb mentality and his cheerful fun-loving disposition. His brain power is history. That fun-loving disposition is somewhat less than history. The lightness of his humors is rather lacking in support. Its existence has been continually asserted but rarely confirmed by evidence.

His only recreation apparently was in changing the character of his mental activities. Madison was a student always. He kept a candle burning by his bedside all night, and his wife said he "slept very little, going to bed late and getting up frequently during the night to write or read."

He was neither an outdoor man nor a man for games, indoor or out, though there is a fugitive reference to his having played chess. His interest in wild life was to weigh the creatures, and measure them, even down to their individual claws, and thus compare the wild animals of America with those of Europe. A particular instance is the meticulous care he took in comparing our monax with the European marmotte. In addition to his measurings and weighings he wanted to find a monax nest in summer, note and mark it, and open it in winter and see if that animal hibernated like the marmotte. He was not interested in guns and hunting knives; but he wrote Jefferson in France, asking for "a portable glass" and compass "with a spring for stopping the vibrations of the needle when not in use." He used his compass to guide him in observing wild life, not in hunting it. A hundred years later Madison would have hunted with a camera.

He seems not even to have had the Virginian's love of a horse. He was rarely on a horse's back, at least after his unrevealed boyhood. He preferred driving to riding, but, even then, a coachman held the reins. He was, as the saying goes, "taken to drive." He seemed not to have that feeling for a horse that makes one want to mount him and move as one with him along the roads and trails, across country, over hedges and fences and ditches. Yet he indulged a fancy for having thoroughbred horses to draw his carriage, and actually owned a race-horse in partnership with merry Doctor Thornton, the architect of the United States Capitol and of many of the best houses and of some of the gayest quips of his day.

Madison usually referred to Montpellier as his "farm," but he was no dirt farmer. He took up the study of law "to avoid becoming a planter." Theories of land and crops he had of course, imposed by his inheritance, and he wrote to his neighbor and mentor, Jefferson, of seeds and soil; but if his beautiful big house and its great acreage had not been left him by his father, it might easily be imagined that Madison would have domiciled himself in a city, and have been happier there.

He lived in a period when a planter contrived and installed his own practical conveniences, or went without them. He had not Franklin's or Jefferson's love for contriving or their facility for tooling. It is known, however, that one of the practical features which he inaugurated on his farm was an ice-house, said to have been the first sunk in that part of Virginia. It is remembered for the wager it occasioned. The country people in the neighborhood would not believe that ice could be kept all summer. Among the doubting Thomases was Madison's own overseer, one Edward Brockman. So, to cure his incredulity, Madison promised his man ice for a mint-julep on the Fourth of July in return for a turkey at Christmas. Ice-houses were certainly well known much earlier in other parts of Virginia.

Madison, though studious, was far from being a recluse. He was fond of human companionship. He was, however, a poor judge of men and had

little capacity for controlling them. The failure
of his Cabinets is evidence of this. Unlike Jefferson, he never shunned discussion, but preferably
courted it. "Copenhagen" Jackson, in spite of his
reflection on the President's personal appearance,
granted that "he had great simplicity of manners"
and was "an inveterate enemy of form and
ceremony."

He was neither silent nor glum, neither uninter-
esting nor a kill-joy. Nevertheless, Gay, one of his
biographers, became bored with Madison; but it
was really only one side of Madison with which he
seems to have become acquainted, the Madison of
the written document, and it is quite true that Madison's pen seldom smiled. Another biographer,
Gaillard Hunt, without supporting his assertions
with too much evidence, found that Madison, at
his receptions, "circulated freely among the people
and was polite to all. When he spoke, no
ponderous words of wisdom fell from his lips, but
he talked and encouraged them to talk, of lighter
things, and occasionally he made remarks which
caused the men to laugh and the women to blush;
for, by a strange contradiction, this man who was
more deeply read than any other of our presidents,
and who knew more about the science and

philosophy of government, was a friviolous humor-
ist in the relaxations of private life, and when the
mood was on him could set the guests about his
table into roars of laughter." Such examples of
Madison's levity as survive seem to indicate that
the truth lies someplace between the gravity of
Gay and the gaiety of Hunt.

Yet the latter was, at second hand, much nearer
right. Margaret Bayard Smith often met Madison
and in her gossipy way reported similar impressions, again without giving the evidence of what
he said. The Secretary of State and his wife came
to call, and "Mr. M. was in one of his most sportive
moods"; she went to his first inaugural ball, and he
came up to her and conversed, and "he made some
of his old kind of mischievous allusions"; years
later she was at a house-party at Montpellier, and
"some of Mr. M's anecdotes were droll, and we
often laughed very heartily. He retains all the
sportiveness of his character, which he used to reveal now and then to those whom he knew inti-
mately, and Mrs. M. says he is as fond of a frolic
and of romping with the girls as ever." One shares
her wish that her letter had been long enough to
contain a few of Madison's droll anecdotes, which,
she tantalizingly added, "I am sure would make

you laugh, too." And how one would like to know more of those "rompings with the girls" which, without support or suggestion in any other single instance in all Madisoniana, may be suspected of being a bit of condescension on the part of the undreading Dolly.

In spite of the limitations of Mrs. Smith's letters, examples of his otherwise little attested lighter moments are not wholly lacking, coming down to us by devious paths. Though some might think them far enough, about the nearest thing to levity that slipped from Mr. Madison's generally sober pen, as distinguished from his conversation, were his reporting of the remarks of Franklin in the Constitutional Convention; a sly Apologue entitled *Jonathan Bull and Mary Bull;* and his rather more spontaneously sprightly letter to the Marquis de LaFayette.

When the great battle for the Constitution was finished, in the first moments of relaxation, while the last members were signing their names thereto, "Dr. Franklin," wrote Madison, "looking towards the President's chair, at the back of which a rising sun happened to be painted, observed to a few members near him that painters had found it difficult to distinguish in their art a rising sun from a setting sun.

" 'I have,' said he, 'often and often, in the course of the session, looked at that behind the President, without being able to tell whether it was rising or setting. But now, at length, I have the happiness to know, that it is a rising sun.' "

Franklin's anecdotes and familiar incidents generally illustrated and fixed in the hearers' minds some profound truth of moral and political science. One such, of half a dozen others which Madison preserved, he told in these terms:

"After the adjournment, the doctor observed to several of us who were near him, in allusion to the poor sample which had been given of human reason, that there was on board a ship, in which he once crossed the Atlantic, a man who had from his birth been without the sense of smelling. On sitting down to dinner one day, one of the mess cut off a piece of beef, and, putting it to his nose, cried out: 'This beef stinks!'

"The one next him, cutting off and smelling a piece, said, 'Not at all, it is as sweet as any meat I ever smelled.'

"A third, passing a piece across his nose several times,—'Stinks,' says he: 'No, I believe not: yes, I believe it does,'—repeating the opposite opinions as often as he made the trial.

"The same doubts and contrarities went round, as the company, one after another, expressed their opinions.

" 'Now, gentlemen,' exclaimed the man without a sense of smelling, 'I am convinced of what I long suspected, that what you call smelling has no existence, and that it is nothing but mere fancy and prejudice.' "

The Apologue already referred to presented the Northern and the Southern States as man and wife, discussing in veiled terms the political issues threatening even then to divide them. The writing of it is assigned to the year 1821, and the race problem is revealed as already one of the acute intersectional issues. Madison veiled it under this metaphor:

"Mary, when a child, had unfortunately received from a certain African dye a stain on her left arm, which made it perfectly black, and withal somewhat weaker than the other arm. The misfortune arose from a ship from Africa, loaded with the article, which had been permitted to enter a river running through her estate, and dispose of a part of the noxious cargo."

Other issues Madison presented similarly, and, at length, concluded with amiable tact, that "the bickerings which had sprung up ended, as the quarrels of lovers always, and of married folks sometimes do, in an increased affection and confidence between the parties."

The end of the letter to LaFayette, dated March, 1785, discloses Madison's pen in one of its least guarded moments: "I received a letter a few days ago from M^r. Mercer, written in the bosom of wedlock at M^r. Sprigg's; another at the same time from Monroe, who was well in New York. I have nothing to say for myself but that I have exchanged Richmond for Orange . . . that I enjoy a satisfactory share of health; that I spend the chief of my time in reading, and the chief of my reading, on Law; that I hear with the greatest pleasure of your being far better employed; and that I am, with most affectionate esteem," etc. etc.

There is another letter which bears the signatures of "W. Ellery," a Rhode Island signer of the Declaration of Independence, and "Js. Madison, Jr." It is written from Philadelphia to Mr. Matthews, of South Carolina, Mr. Peabody, of New Hampshire, and General Schuyler, of New York, three Members sent as a Congressional Committee to the Army Headquarters in the field. Its irresponsible manner witnesses the youth of which-

ever of the owners of the two names subscribed
was responsible for the concoction. It is dated "In
Congress, May 5, 1780," and frolics along in this
mannered fashion:

"Ye poor devils! shivering on the bleak hills of
Morris, how we pity you!—Ho! soldier with your
canteen;—view that poor committeeman—see him
trembling. Hark!—hear his teeth chatter—unable
to support himself under the chilling blasts, which,
unclothed and unfed, you have endured with in-
vincible perseverence and fortitude:—see him
expiring!—he was nursed under a fervid sun, and
exposes himself to your nipping gales to bring you
some relief. For the sake of G—d, one drop of
whiskey for poor Matthews!

"As for ye sons of the North, ye can get along
well enough, especially, if ye can find, now and
then, a cup of beer and a little New England.

"As for our illustrious general, if it were in our
own choice, for him the rich Madeira should flow
in copious streams;—and as for the gallant officers,
and faithful brave soldiers under his command, if
we had the power of conversion, we would turn
water into wine, the camp should overflow with
that exhilarating and invigorating liquor.

"The last bottle had been broached.—We addressed Congress, and used every argument in our power to induce them to order a couple of pipes to be sent to headquarters, and told them that the general's wine was entirely exhausted. They doubted. We informed them that we had received a letter from the committee giving us that information. They still doubted, and desired that the letter might be produced. We delivered it with the utmost reluctance. Upon reading it, congress immediately concluded that any persons that would charge us with niggardliness, and threaten to run congress 'd——ly' in debt must be 'd——ly' drunk, and utterly refused to send any wine to headquarters until you should have returned. We wish you had been more guarded in your expressions.— However, we shall for once stretch our power, and send you two pipes immediately.—You will be pleased to consider soberly the business you have undertaken, and the expectations of congress, and not drink more than three glasses of wine at dinner, and six at supper; and whenever you write to us, do it before breakfast.

"We return your 'word to the wise,' and are your's as you conduct."

One of Madison's favorite anecdotes was about Jefferson, and another was about Ben Harrison.

Madison and Jefferson made a trip through the Northern States, nearly to the Canadian line, in the year 1791. In New York they were the central figures at a dinner when, as every where at the time, the operation of the new Constitution was the subject of conversation. Madison recalled that, at that dinner, a good deal was said about the desirability of having an hereditary executive as against an elective one; and, after one speaker had revealed himself long and strong against the agitations and animosities of a popular choice, Madison said that "Mr. Jefferson, with a smile remarked that he had heard of a university somewhere, in which the Professor of Mathematics was hereditary."

His way of telling the Harrison story was after this fashion: "While a member of the first Congress, which met in Philadelphia, he [Harrison] was on one occasion joined by a friend as he left the congressional hall. Wishing to ask his friend to join him in a bumper, he took him to a certain place where supplies were furnished to the members of Congress, and called for two glasses of brandy-and-water. The man in charge replied that liquors were not included in supplies furnished to Congressmen.

"'Why,' asked Harrison, 'what is it then that

I see the New England members come here and drink?'

" 'Molasses and water, which they have charged as *stationary,*' was the reply.

" 'Very well,' said Harrison, 'give me the brandy-and-water, and charge it as *fuel.*' "

Madison did not spare himself when he offered a witticism. Though Marshall's equal mentally, he was physically the antithesis of that splendid figure, and his slight frame and poor health kept him out of the war. But he used laughingly to claim that he had nevertheless received "his scar in defense of his country." It happened the year he and Monroe campaigned against each other for a seat in the first Congress of the newly federated United States. He told Trist:

"We used to meet in days of considerable excitement and address the people on our respective sides; but there was never an atom of ill-will between us. On one occasion we met at a church up here [pointing to the northwest]. There was a nest of Dutchmen in that quarter, who generally went together, and whose vote might very probably turn the scale. We met there at church. Service was performed, and then they had music with two fiddles. They are remarkably fond of music.

When it was all over we addressed the people, and kept them standing in the snow listening to the discussion of constitutional subjects. They stood it out very patiently—seemed to consider it a sort of fight of which they were required to be the spectators. I then had to ride in the night, twelve miles to quarters, and got my nose frost-bitten, of which I bear the mark now." Then pointing to the scar on the left side of his nose, he would laugh and claim it as "his scar of a wound received in defense of his country."

Another man he met in similar discussions was his neighbor, Governor James Barbour. There were two Barbour brothers, Phil and James, and John Randolph said of their relative capacity as debaters: "Phil Barbour aims at a horse-hair and splits it, James aims at a barn door and misses it." Yet, an Orange farmer, who had heard Madison and Governor James address the crowd on Court Day, when asked which of those two was the greater, said: "Barbour! Barbour is so great a man that I did not understand a word he said. I understood every word Madison said, and he didn't tell me anything I don't know."

Madison sometimes poked fun at his own lack of capacity for foreign languages, though, as a matter of fact, he had a mastery of Greek and Latin, corresponded with Mazzei and Bellini in Italian, and had studied French. But he told of an early use of what he called his Scotch-French which added nothing to its record for practical service.

A Frenchman came to Princeton and called on the president of the college. Madison was a student at the time, and as he was the only known "French scholar" there, he was called in by the president as interpreter. When he appeared the Frenchman began to hold forth at him. Madison said that, listening with all his might, he was able to catch a few words, enough to pick out a shred of the other's meaning. Communicating this to the president, Madison's turn came and he launched forth in what he thought was French. But it became evident to him, and to every one else present, that the poor Frenchman did not understand a single word that he was saying.

"I might as well," said Madison, "have been talking Kickapoo at him! I had learnt French of my Scotch tutor, reading it with him as we did Greek and Latin; that is, as a dead language; and this, too, pronounced with a Scotch accent, which was quite broad, and a twang of which my own tongue had probably caught."

He still made himself the butt of his own jokes at the other end of his long life. Once when the doctor came to Montpellier he found Madison out of bed and lying on a sofa, chatting with some ladies. When the doctor reproved him and told him that he should have to lie still, he answered: "Oh, well, I talk most easily when I lie."

It was under similar circumstances, while he was lying on his couch during another of the doctor's visits, with the door open into the dining-room where the doctor was at table with the family, that Madison cried out with a feeble but frolicsome voice: "Doctor, are you pushing about the bottle? Do your duty, Doctor, or I must cashier you."

The two great friendships of Madison's life were with Thomas Jefferson and with Dolly Madison, his wife. He was twenty-five when he first met Jefferson. They were neighbors in the Virginia hill country, their houses having a distance of only twenty-five miles between them, but they had not met until they came together as members of the first revolutionary legislature of their colony, in 1776. Then began a friendship which continued without abatement for fifty years and terminated only with Jefferson's death. Their correspondence fills volumes. Madison has been called Jefferson's political stepson. Theirs was certainly one of the unique examples of the friendship of great historical characters. As his end approached, Jefferson wrote Madison: "To myself you have been a pillar of support through life. Take care of me when dead, and be sure that I shall leave with you my last affections."

When Madison and the sprightly widow, Dorothea Payne Todd, were married, though he was in his forty-fourth year, she was in her twenty-sixth. She became his constant and unrivaled love in marriage, but she was not the first woman to stir his affections.

There was in Philadelphia, in 1783, a light-hearted beauty from New York, Catherine Floyd, whose father signed the Declaration of Independence for his state, and she promised to marry Madison. But she found him "sickly, short, and not good-looking," nor had she before her a man who had yet raised himself to any particular eminence; and, moreover, there was a young clergyman in Philadelphia "hanging around her at the harpsichord"; so the next thing Madison knew he received his dismissal in a letter "sealed with a piece of rye dough." The reason for this kind of seal is still waiting for an explanation. Poor Madison confided his grief to Jefferson, who consoled him "with philosophy." She married "the other man," and Madison continued his climb to greatness.

No names were mentioned, but in 1786, Henry Lee, Jr., none other than General "Lighthorse Harry," wrote him: "You continued a long time in Phila^{da} we hear, this unexpected movement gives eye to various suggestions all tending to prove that you are in full gallop to the blessed yoke." The charmer in this case remains a mystery.

Eleven years passed, after the passing of Catherine Floyd, before he actually met his sentimental fate. Among them were the most absorbing and significant years of his life for Madison, for he not only seized opportunity as it passed, but made opportunity and realized on it to the limit during this period. After these eleven years he was no longer the insignificant Madison whose dismissal was sealed with rye dough. He had become the celebrated builder and defender of the Constitution, one of the greatest men on this continent.

And then along came Dolly. She was in Philadelphia, too, and recently a widow. At twenty-six

Dorothea Payne Todd was one of the most vivacious belles in the capital, a character she seems to have maintained to the end of her eighty-five vivacious years. The fame of Madison was dinning in her ears, and he, at this point, seems to have remarked her charm, for presently she wrote a friend: "Aaron Burr says that the great little Madison has asked to be brought to see me." He came, and she conquered, and capitulated, too; and there followed forty-one years of unclouded married life.

There is an impression that Dolly made Madison. She helped him. She helped him enormously with the social side of his later public life, but she never made him anything but happy. Madison made himself, and completed the job before he ever met the Widow Todd. It is true that after his marriage he became Secretary of State and had his two terms as President, but he extended his achievements thereby no farther than he had by his preeminent performances for the Constitution. So far as achievement went, the rest of his career was something of an anti-climax. Dolly became the heroine of a not quite superfluous last act, although a charming, dainty, darling, delightful, gracious, ringletted, furbelowed, turbaned, heroine, whom

every one admired and loved and made much of,
but none more than her great little husband.

She was all personality and so she eclipsed
Madison's unimpressive externals. She never so
much as discussed politics or politicians, much less
interfered in policies and appointments, but she
made friends with every one who came near her
and probably made them the President's friends,
too, and, to that extent, proved an invaluable social
aide.

The gossipy historians who mentioned the
Madisons talked of Dolly to the comparative ex-
clusion of James. She became "Queen Dolly," but
no one seems ever to have thought of her husband
as "King James." From all accounts of the two
characters, the mature, retiring, adoring husband
might be said to have been content to keep his
personality in his wife's name. In retirement at
Montpellier, however, they appeared to have struck
a more nearly balanced average.

"I spent 2 days with M^r and Mrs Madison—
they inquired kindly after you. Her soul is as big
as ever and her body has not decreased. M^r M is
the picture of happiness they look like Adam and
Eve in Paradise." So, after leaving Montpellier,
wrote a friend to Eliza Lee. The Madisons had

then been out of the public eye for two whole years. He was sixty-eight, she was fifty-one. Perhaps, by that time, a shade less like Adam and Eve than like Darby and Joan.

There was only one cloud. The happy pair were childless. Perhaps a trifle worse than that even, for in the offing, always a little menacing, was the wretched dissipated son of Dolly's first marriage.

Life at Montpellier at that time was easy though not opulent. Madison was not rich. His colored body-servant gossiped afterward, not unkindly, saying that his master, who dressed wholly in black—the buff and blue suit seems to have had its day—with silk stockings and with buckles on his shoes and breeches—"never had but one suit at a time," because "he had some poor relatives that he had to help, and wished to set them an example of economy in the matter of dress."

But they entertained in the friendly, open-handed, open-house planter style; sometimes, as had Washington and Jefferson, feeling the burden of the visits of curious strangers who came to see the great man to whom the other patriots had been a vivid intimate experience. But, when he spoke of the long line of visitors over that last quarter of a century in retirement, he was uncomplaining. He admitted that "some were bounties" even if "others were taxes."

Family they always had with them. Rather more of Dolly's came than Madison's. Washington similarly had found himself surrounded almost altogether with the former Widow Custis's connections at Mount Vernon. At least once the Madisons splurged, and invited the whole county to come to Montpellier, but the great house was much too small for the vast gathering. So the party was made into a picnic, and there were tables all over the lawns; and Mistress Dolly was everywhere, attending to everything, making every one welcome and comfortable, bringing out every one, with her undisputed genius for making a party "go"; though the most we hear of Mr. Madison is that he moved among his guests "speaking with every one."

For nearly a decade there were fortnightly drives, some twenty-five miles south, to visit Mr. Jefferson, "for a day or two," and sometimes longer, at Monticello. But those fell off when Jefferson died, on July fourth, 1826. Soon word came down from Massachusetts that John Adams had passed away on that identical Fourth of July, at almost the same hour as had Jefferson. Curiously, not long after, on another Fourth of July, only five years later, another of the old guard who helped to free the colonies and make our nation, James Monroe, went to his last sleep.

Madison was beginning to feel his isolation. In 1831 he was the sole surviving signer of the Constitution; nor was there alive any other member of the Convention who was present but did not sign. "I happen, also," he wrote in that same year, "to be the sole survivor of those who were members of the Revolutionary Congress prior to the close of the war; as I had been, for some years, of the members of the Convention in 1776, which formed the first Constitution for Virginia." And then he added: "Having outlived so many of my contemporaries, I ought not to forget that I may be thought to have outlived myself."

The fathers were not unconscious of the parts they had played in founding the Republic, nor of the splendid isolation into which the passing of the years raised the survivors. How they thought of the period they had helped to make historic was in one instance uncovered by Jefferson, in a letter presenting his grandson to John Adams:

"Like other young people, he wishes to be able

JAMES MADISON

in the winter night of old age, to recount to those
around him, what he has heard and learnt of the
heroic age preceding his birth, and which of the
Argonauts individually he was in time to have
seen."

Madison outlived them all. He was the last
survivor of "the heroic age," the last of those
American "Argonauts."

THE END

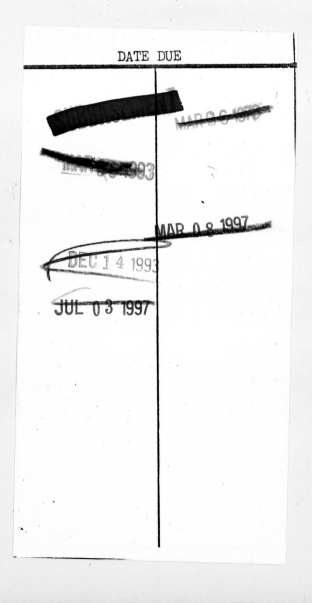